how to grow
GIANT
vegetables

how to grow
GIANT
vegetables

bernard lavery

photography by
stephen daniels

HarperPerennial
A Division of HarperCollins*Publishers*

Author's Acknowledgments

I would like to thank Mr Ray Waterman of Collins, New York, the
President of the World Pumpkin Federation, for providing me with his
pumpkin seed and fund of knowledge, which undoubtedly laid the
foundation stone for my 'giant kingdom'. My sincere gratitude is also offered
to Mr Norris McWhirter, co-founder of the *Guinness Book of Records*, for
his assistance and encouragement over many years.
I am also most grateful to my literary agent, Mrs Caroline Davidson
for her patience and commitment to this book, and to the photographer
Stephen Daniels for providing its many excellent photographs.
Finally, a huge thank you to everyone at HarperCollins who have
made the publication of this book possible.

This book was originally published in the United Kingdom in 1995 by HarperCollins*Publishers*

FIRST U.S. EDITION

ISBN 0-06-095191-5

96 97 98 99 00 XXX 10 9 8 7 6 5 4 3 2 1

For HarperCollins *Publishers*:
Editorial Director Polly Powell
Project Editor Carole McGlynn
Art Director Ray Barnett
Designer Rachel Smythe
Production Controller Bridget Scanlon

Edited by Caroline Taylor

Design by Arthur Brown
for Cooling Brown *(Book Packaging)*, 9-11 High Street
Hampton, Middlesex TW12 2SA

Illustrations: David Thelwell

Archive photography courtesy of The Hulton Deutsch Picture Library

contents

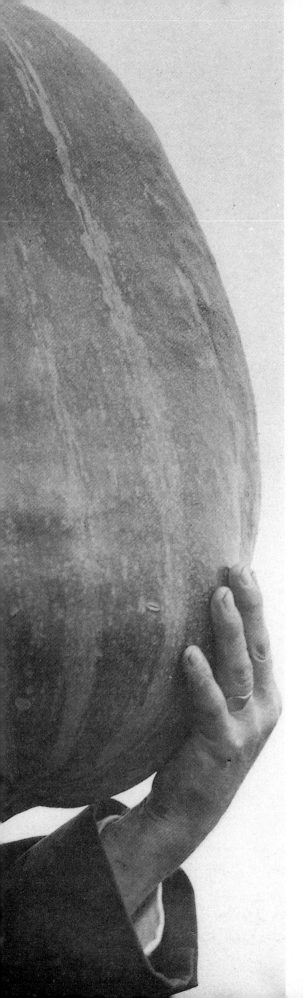

foreword

The competitive growing of fruits and vegetables has a history as long as that of the village flower and vegetable show. The first such was recorded at Dannybrook, County Cork, Ireland, in 1817. In some regions there are particular traditions and elaborate rules – the most famous being that of the Northumbrian pot leek. In 1987 there was intense excitement over the whole of Geordieland when Mr Harrigan of Linton broke through the 12lb barrier.

The dimensions or weights of some categories have to be seen to be believed, culminating in a pumpkin from Ontario, Canada, weighing well over a third of a ton. The tale is told of a keen grower of outsize redcurrants who was bitterly disappointed at his failure to carry off the local prize, until he learned that his exhibit had been misidentified and received third prize in the tomato section!

Of all growers, the one who strikes most awe in his rivals is the author of this book, Bernard Lavery. In the autumn of 1989, Garden News recorded the name of the new star from Llanharry, Mid Glamorgan, alongside six new records, including a 124lb cabbage, a 12ft 8in parsnip and a 6cwt 38lb pumpkin. In 1990, Bernard was back, not merely with United Kingdom records, but World Records in four new categories, including a 108lb marrow and a 46lb celery. In this pioneer work of reference he reveals the story behind and the techniques involved in growing his record-breaking, outsize vegetables.

Norris McWhirter

Norris McWhirter

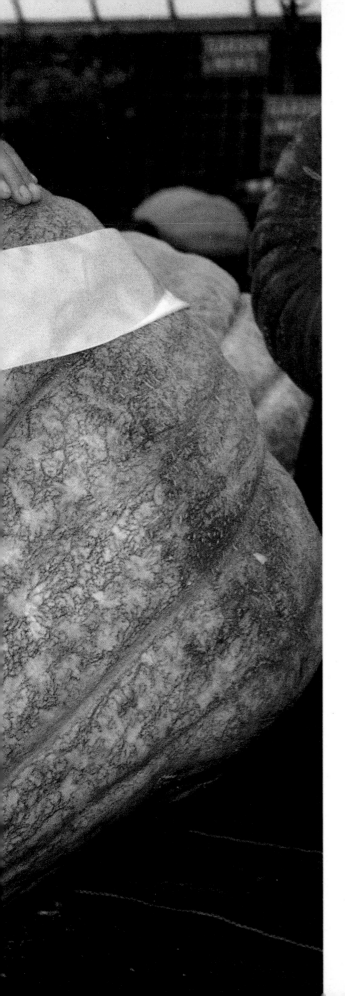

introduction

"I remember vividly how my journey into the unknown world of giant vegetables all started. I was already growing vegetables for exhibition, and one cold winter's night was sitting with my family in front of a big log fire, drawing up plans for the forthcoming season's vegetable garden…"

This prize-winning marrow (right) was entered by a local allotment association in the Victory Garden Show of Vegetables held to celebrate the end of the Second World War in 1945.

Can you imagine a carrot measuring 16ft 10½ in (5.14m) long, the equivalent of seven normal walking paces of an adult? Or a radish weighing 28lb 1oz (12.7kg), the combined weight of four average-sized newborn babies? It may be even harder to visualize a 124lb (56kg) cabbage – enough to feed a family twice a week for a whole year – or a head of celery weighing 46lb (21kg), fifty times bigger than a normal one. Would you believe your eyes if you saw a parsnip 14ft 3in (4.34m) long – about the length of a family car), or a massive cucumber 24in (60cm) long and 18in (45cm) round, enough to make cucumber sandwiches for a whole summer? You may even consider that a 108lb (49kg) vegetable marrow measuring over 36in (90cm) long would be an impossibility, not to mention a pumpkin 4ft (1.20m) high and 13ft 2in (4m) in circumference, weighing 710lb (322kg).

Geoff Capes, who held the strongest man record for many years, inspects a monster onion.

Incredible or impossible, these were the weights and measurements of nine of my World Records established before 1992.

The idea of growing bigger and better vegetables has been around since Cain started tilling the land. Farmers are pleased when their yields are higher than average; most gardeners are excited when an exceptionally large specimen of any vegetable suddenly appears. I call it 'the magic of nature'.

From a very early age I was fascinated with tales of 'monster' pumpkins, but when as a child I was taken to see my first pantomime, 'Cinderella', I thought the scene about a pumpkin turning into a coach a bit far-fetched. There was no way anyone could get inside a pumpkin; pumpkins were just not big enough. I was soon, of course, to be proved wrong.

Getting started

I remember vividly how my journey into the unknown world of giant vegetables all began. I was already growing vegetables for exhibition, and one cold winter's night was sitting with my family in front of a big log fire, drawing up plans for the forthcoming season's vegetable garden. Without warning my youngest son, John, said, 'Dad, can you grow me a big pumpkin?' My immediate answer was, 'What a good idea', and I saw his eyes light up like bright stars. Perhaps mine did, too. Certainly, from that moment on I looked forward to spring and the coming challenge as never before.

Throughout that season we tended our pumpkin plant with loving care, and at harvest time we were pleased as Punch with our 120lb (54kg) pumpkin. Six years later, when I broke the world record with one weighing 710lb (322kg), I thought it was the eighth wonder of the world; I cannot describe the joy it gave me and my family to feel that we had grown the heaviest pumpkin in the whole world. I was also sure that if it had turned into Cinderella's coach, at least two people could have sat inside it quite comfortably.

The taste of giants

The belief some people have that very large or giant vegetables are tasteless is, I assure you, totally inaccurate. If specimens are over-mature, their taste and quality may well deteriorate, but this of course is true of 'normal' sized vegetables. When giants are at their peak and freshly harvested, most taste truly magnificent.

Interest is spreading

Growing vegetables for home consumption has always been one of man's pursuits, either out of necessity or as a hobby. Now that seeds of giant varieties are readily available, a whole new experience is within everyone's reach. Young gardeners throughout the world are taking up the hobby, and new clubs and associations are being formed to accommodate the growing number of giant vegetable enthusiasts. Most of the major horticultural shows now cater for a complete range of giant vegetables, and although climates differ greatly from country to country, the reported results are amazing. America has traditionally been the home of big vegetables, but the enthusiasm for growing giants has now spread to Canada as well as to

Bernard Lavery with his vegetable display at the 1994 Giant Vegetable Show held at Baytree Nursery in Spalding, England.

Europe, Africa, Asia and Australasia.

Growing giant vegetables is fun, it is easy, and anyone can do it. Giant pumpkins, squash and marrows will increase in size by 2–3in (5–7cm) a day, and will seem to grow even as you watch. What better way could there be to capture the horticultural imagination of a youngster?

How is it done?

How can *you* grow vegetables the size of those illustrated here? There are three essentials: firstly, you need good quality seeds that have the genetic potential to grow giants. Secondly, you need to provide ideal growing conditions and follow the methods that I describe in this book. And lastly, you must pray for good weather and for Lady Luck to sit on your shoulder throughout the growing season.

Seeds and selection

Seed breeding has always held a fascination for me, and I have been involved with it for as long as I can remember. I am continually trying to improve and breed new varieties of vegetables, and I have developed many new strains that have broken world records. However, in this book I will tell you both how to obtain bigger and better results from your ordinary seed packets, and how to amaze yourself and your friends by growing 'monsters' to record-breaking standards, using specialist seeds.

Respecting nature

I have had tremendous pleasure and success from my seed-breeding activities, and from

experimenting with cultivation techniques, but I do not mind admitting that I have had my share of failures as well. Nature is a great leveller. It does not matter how much knowledge you have, or how clever you think you are;

The best way to buy seeds is at the shows, where specialist growers will be exhibiting, or by mail order.

nature will cut you down to size if you do not respect her demands. It is terminal for a plant if you get things wrong, and since you only get one chance in a year, you will have to wait until the next season to try something different. Success, however, more than makes up for all the disappointments along the way.

My secrets disclosed

I have so far collected eighteen world records for my giants, but the exciting thing is that there is always something new to be discovered. I am still looking for improvements throughout the whole range of vegetables.

In this book I disclose all the tips, 'secrets' and new growing techniques that I have discovered over the years, so that you may have a whole new gardening experience at your fingertips. If, however, you are already a world record holder I have some advice for you: enjoy the glory while you can, for every reader of this book will be a potential world record-breaker within a very short space of time!

I hope you enjoy reading this book and that you will have many years of pleasure growing giant vegetables. I have certainly enjoyed disclosing my 'secrets', and hope that the experience which I have accumulated over many years in the field of the giants will be helpful to you.

One further piece of advice: do not despair if you do not break any world records at your first attempt. So long as your annual results are your personal best, you will always be a winner!

Bernard Lavery

Bernard Lavery

Bernard Lavery with a freshly harvested white mooli radish.

chapter one

preparation and planning

When planning your giant vegetable garden you should take into account your financial limits; the types of vegetable you would like to grow; the total area involved; the exposure of your plot; the type and structure of your soil; and whether to use a polythene growing tunnel or glasshouse.

Giant vegetables to suit your pocket

Growing some giant vegetables to record-breaking standards can be quite expensive, but the majority will be well within the reach of most gardeners' pockets. I have separated the vegetables into four different categories, according to the cost of growing them:

Expensive Onions and leeks. For these a heated glasshouse or polythene growing tunnel and heat will be required for the winter and early spring months, in countries where night-time temperatures fall below 50° F (10° C).

Moderate cost

Tomatoes, cucumbers and melons. In many areas a glasshouse or growing tunnel will be required, but these subjects can be grown outdoors once the danger of night-time frost has passed.

Inexpensive Cabbages, parsnips, carrots, radishes, swedes, beetroots, and any other root vegetables. All can be grown in open ground.
Optional Pumpkins, squash and marrows. These vegetables can be grown either under cover or outside.

I must admit that I spend more than the average person on my garden, but my excuse is that most hobbies cost money, and the amount of pleasure that I derive from it is incalculable. And what other hobby can provide the whole family with a constant supply of big, fresh, delicious vegetables?

Seed selection

Selecting seeds for the coming season is, for me, one of the most exciting times of the horticultural year; I spend hours searching through catalogues and stores for new varieties of seed to try. Gone are last year's successes, mistakes and failures, and once again I look forward to the challenge of a new season.

It is important to select varieties of seed which have the genetic capability to grow big; that is to say, seed which comes from giant strains. The chances of growing a 500lb

An airman arrives for an annual horticultural show in 1947 with his giant marrow and pumpkin.

Breaking the Barrier

Large pumpkins have been grown and exhibited competitively for centuries and until the beginning of the 1980s nobody had broken the 500lb (226kg) barrier. In 1984 a contest organized by the World Pumpkin Federation offered cash prizes to the first person to grow a 500lb (226kg) pumpkin: four growers in the United States topped this weight and one made it to the 600lb (270kg) mark. In 1989 Bernard Lavery grew a 710lb (322kg) specimen and held the record for three days before being outclassed by a Canadian. And already the 1,000lb (450kg) barrier is in sight.

(226kg) pumpkin with seed from a 100lb (45kg) one is very slim indeed. Seed from giant strains is now available from seed catalogues, shops and garden centres around the world, but best of all is to find a supplier with a reputation for growing 'giants', who is willing to sell you seed from his prize specimens.

The germination of these seeds is also a crucial moment in the gardener's year, and unfortunately the success rate varies every time. So I always sow twice as many seeds as I will need plants, believing it better to have too many seedlings than not enough. This insurance policy is well worth the cost of that extra packet of seeds.

Planning the layout

Planning maximum efficiency from your giants' vegetable garden will probably present you with the biggest jigsaw puzzle of your life. The first thing you need to do is to work out the total growing area you have at your disposal,

either in the open ground or in a glasshouse or tunnel. At the beginning of each chapter I give a recommended area for the optimum growth of one plant of the vegetable concerned, and from this you will be able to work out which plants you have room to grow, and how many of each variety. On page 18 I describe a crop rotation method which is designed to ensure that you make the most of the soil you have for the benefit of your giants.

Armed with this information and your budget limits for the season, you can design your own layout and finalize plans. It is ideal if your garden faces south and enjoys the sun for most of a cloudless day, but do not worry too much if it does not; nature has its own ways of adjusting to such things as shaded gardens.

Glasshouse or polythene tunnel?

If you intend to erect a glasshouse or polythene growing tunnel, there are several points to consider before you choose which to purchase.

The expected life of a glasshouse before any major maintenance is required is usually about twelve years. The life of a growing tunnel is similar, but a new polythene cover will be needed every three years. It is better to change an old cover after this period, even if it looks intact, since you could lose everything inside if an old cover were to tear in a winter's storm.

To work out comparative costs, divide the purchase price of a glasshouse by the total squared measurement of the ground inside it. Do the same for a tunnel, but add the price of three extra

These giant marrow seeds are shown here at approximately half their actual size.

covers. You will probably find that the cost per square foot or metre of the tunnel will be less than that of the glasshouse, but the tunnel may be less attractive to look at, and the glasshouse will be more efficient to manage, and temperatures easier to control. Thereafter, the choice is yours!

Wind protection

Prevailing or damaging winds must be taken into account when planning your garden. If you intend to operate without covers, then some form of wind shield will be essential, and the most effective is one made from a very fine plastic mesh. This will break up the wind's force without causing as much resistance or turbulence as a solid sheet of plastic or polythene. If you are erecting a glasshouse or polythene growing tunnel, remember that the strongest part is the end, so a multi-structural one should be erected end-on to the most severe winds. However, a single span tunnel or glasshouse should be quite safe sited at the edge of the garden with its longest side facing

Young carrots are seen growing in a raised bed easily constructed from old timber. This ensures that the best soil is used and cannot be compacted.

the direction of the wind. It will also give protection to other tender plants within the confines of the garden itself.

Soil preparation

There are so many different types and structures of soil that it would be impossible for me to feature them all individually in this book.

An ideal soil consists of 12in (30cm) of good topsoil on top of a free-draining subsoil, and there are some lucky gardeners who have just this combination. At the other end of the spectrum there are the unfortunate ones who have soil of a clay-type structure with poor drainage. I therefore give only a broad outline to soil preparation.

Humus is the key to success

Most vegetables need as much humus or organic matter incorporated into the soil as

crop rotation plan

Roughly one quarter of the total area should be allocated for brassicas (which includes cabbages, swedes and radishes) and each year this area should move round by a quarter of a turn. The section which previously had brassicas planted in it can be used for pumpkins, marrows, leeks, onions and runner beans during the following two years. During the fourth year, it will be ideal for growing root crops such as carrots, parsnips, beetroot and celery. By this method, brassicas are grown in the same soil only once in four years.

first year

BRASSICAS
Cabbages
Swedes
Radishes

ROOT CROPS
Carrots
Parsnips
Beetroot
Celery

Pumpkins, Marrows, Squash
Water Melon, Leeks, Onions
Runner Beans

second year

Pumpkins
Marrows
Squash
Water Melon
Leeks
Onions
Runner Beans

BRASSICAS
Cabbages
Swedes
Radishes

ROOT CROPS
Carrots
Parsnips
Beetroot
Celery

fourth year

ROOT CROPS
Carrots
Parsnips
Beetroot
Celery

Pumpkins
Marrows
Squash
Water Melon
Leeks
Onions
Runner Beans

BRASSICAS
Cabbages
Swedes
Radishes

third year

Pumpkins, Marrows, Squash
Water Melon, Leeks, Onions
Runner Beans

ROOT CROPS
Carrots
Parsnips
Beetroot
Celery

BRASSICAS
Cabbages
Swedes
Radishes

possible. It is easy to do this by digging in heaps of farmyard manure in the autumn, and allowing it to rot down during the winter months. If you do not have access to farmyard manure, composted organic materials and peat or a peat substitute will be an excellent alternative.

In judging giant marrows, good condition is considered as important as weight.

Raised beds versus double digging

Many gardening books recommend double digging the vegetable plot. I would only advise this where the topsoil has become compacted or where you need to improve poor drainage. Double digging looks very good on paper, but more often than not subsoil gets mixed with the topsoil and, instead of being improved, the soil structure actually deteriorates. Try to avoid compacting the soil in the first place by laying planks of wood on the ground to walk on.

Best of all, however, when growing record-breaking vegetables, is the use of raised beds, which will give a plant's roots extra growing depth before reaching the cultivated soil underneath. Raised beds can be of any size you wish and can be made from old timber or, as I

prefer, a discarded 45 gallon (200 litre) plastic drum. With the top and bottom removed and the drum cut in half, you will be left with two tubes that will make a pair of excellent raised beds approximately 22in (50cm) deep. If these are placed in position on top of cultivated soil, and filled with a good growing mixture, they will be like five-star hotels for your lucky plants.

Rotation plans

To achieve the best results from your soil it is advisable to use a crop rotation method. This simply means not growing the same crop in the same spot year after year, which will help to prevent nutrients in the soil from becoming unbalanced, and also prevent a build-up of those pests and diseases which thrive on particular plants. An easy way to achieve this is to divide your outdoor growing area into three sections and simply have a three-year cycle. However, if you are growing pumpkins and trailing marrows, which take up far more space

19

The best means of transportation for giant pumpkins is to use a strong canvas sheet and as many able-bodied helpers as the weight demands.

than other vegetables, I suggest that you divide it into four equal sections, excluding any glasshouses or polythene tunnels, and rotate it as shown on the previous page.

Liming

Throughout this book I endeavour to keep things easy to follow and try to avoid technicalities. However, the use of the term pH is, I am afraid, unavoidable. The pH level of your soil indicates whether it is acid or alkaline, and, since different plants need different pH levels for optimum growth, you will need to test the soil and adjust it – by adding lime to increase the alkalinity or organic matter to reduce it.

The crop rotation method can be used to group vegetables that require different pH levels, and the routine I follow is this: each year I lime a different quarter of the total growing

area, and into this quarter will go those plants that require the most alkaline soil. In the first year I will grow brassicas; in the second and third year, as the alkalinity diminishes, pumpkins, marrows, leeks and onions; and in the fourth year, rootcrops with the addition of plenty of organic matter. I then repeat the cycle over again.

I usually check the pH levels in each part of the garden a few weeks before transplanting my seedlings into the ground. You can buy pH test kits at any garden centre; they are easy to use and you can then add lime or organic matter as required in readiness for the plants. I indicate the optimum pH level for each vegetable in the relevant chapter, but do not be too concerned if your soil is a little out – it is not critical.

Feeding your plants

Throughout this book you will find reference to different compound mixtures of fertilizer with the ratios after the letters N, P, K. The N represents nitrogen, for leaf growth, the P represents phosphorous, for root development, and the K stands for potash which strengthens a plant's resistance to disease and will also assist in the ripening process of fruit and vegetables. They may be used in varying proportions.

Lost among the giant pumpkins...

Spraying

To attain the best results in your garden or glasshouse, you must have a regular spraying programme. There are hundreds of differently named products on sale throughout the world, which will be able to deal with the whole range of pests and diseases which may trouble you from time to time throughout a growing season. It is important to read the labels on the containers very carefully, before purchasing, to ensure that the chemical is suitable for spraying on to the kind of crops which you are growing. It is also advisable to wear a mask or filter breathing pad when applying spray, and essential to wash your hands thoroughly once the job is completed.

pumpkins and squash

Pumpkins and squash are very easy to grow and should finish up with a growing stem as thick as your wrist, and each leaf as big as a coffee table, standing 3–4ft (90–120cm) above the soil.

Pumpkins and squash were discovered on the American continent in the sixteenth century. They are members of the ever-increasing cucurbit or gourd family, and first attained international acclaim at the turn of the century when the late William Warnock of Goderich, Ontario, in Canada sent a 400lb (181kg) specimen to the Paris World's Fair in 1900. This first-ever giant was awarded a special bronze medal and diploma from the French Government, and the occasion was the forerunner of today's vigorously contested worldwide competitions. Growing pumpkins and squash has, without doubt,

In 1949, Flt. Lieut. Sharpe flew in to London specially with his giant pumpkin 'Wizard' to show at the Horticultural Halls, Westminster.

been the most fascinating and enjoyable part of my gardening career.

The difference between a pumpkin and a squash, as defined by the World Pumpkin Confederation for exhibition purposes, is that a pumpkin should be cream or light yellow to orange, and a squash green to grey or mottled. They are grown in exactly the same way, so throughout this book I will use the word pumpkin to avoid repetition.

Although pumpkins grow to an enormous size, the timescale from sowing the seed to harvest is quite short, usually about 135 days, or four and a half months. This makes it easy to plan your seed sowing date, especially if you require one for a show or special event. You may ask what on earth you could do with a 500lb (226kg) or 600lb (272kg) pumpkin. Pumpkins are excellent as fund raisers for charity ('Guess the

A pumpkin weighing a staggering 990lb (445.5kg) was grown in 1994 by Mr Herman Bax in Brockville, Ottawa, Canada.

Weight' is my favourite); they make excellent wine; you can boil, steam, microwave, bake, roast, fry or mash them; you can cook them with cream, butter, herbs, sweet spices, rum or brandy. There are dozens of different recipes – both sweet and sour – for pumpkin bread, muffins, cakes, pancakes, pickle, pasta, jam, soup and of course pumpkin pie. Try some of the recipes I give at the end of the chapter.

Planning ahead

Pumpkin plants certainly take up more space than any other vegetable in the garden, so you need to allocate this before drawing up final plans for the giant vegetable garden as a whole. You must decide how many to grow, and therefore how much space to allow, and whether you are going to grow them in the open garden, in a polythene growing tunnel or in a large glasshouse.

The minimum amount of space you need for a plant growing outdoors is about 16ft x 8ft (5m x 2.5m); and for plants grown under cover, about 14ft x 6ft (4.25m x 1.80m). More space will not produce larger pumpkins.

Pumpkins can be grown either outdoors, or indoors in a glasshouse or polythene growing tunnel. Since both methods have advantages and disadvantages I avoid putting all my eggs in one basket and always grow some outside and a few under cover.

Growing indoors

In a poor summer plants in a polythene growing tunnel or glasshouse will be protected from cold or damaging winds, and from the late spring and early autumn frosts which some countries experience. There will, however, be no natural rainfall to wash the dust from the plant's leaves, or to water the roots as only Mother Nature can, and plants may suffer from heat stress.

Even with the ends open, the amount of heat generated inside a polythene growing tunnel in half an hour's full midsummer sunshine has to be experienced to be believed, and these sudden rises in temperature can damage your plants beyond repair. If the root systems dry out, the plant's leaves will wilt like wet washing on a clothes line, and although they will pick up again when you water the plant, or when the temperature drops at night, your pumpkin will have had a check. The plant itself may appear to revive completely, but the results will show later, when the pumpkin matures prematurely before reaching its full potential. At worst, the sap in the leaves will boil up, leaving the leaves brittle and useless.

To prevent sun scorch of this kind, you either have to be on hand at all times, or use some form of shading on your glass or polythene. I spray an anti-glare product on my glass and polythene in the summer months; this allows the brightness to penetrate but lowers the temperature by 10–15° F (5–8° C), and I wash this shading off with a soft sweeping brush and a hosepipe when the growing season is over. On an extremely hot day it is also beneficial to spray the pumpkin plants with warm water: fill a 45 gallon (200 litre) drum with water from the mains and let the sun do the work of warming it up. If you are out at work all day in the growing season, leave the doors (or doors and windows) half open or, if a strong wind is blowing, the lee side door alone.

Growing outdoors

Growing pumpkins outdoors is a far less expensive exercise in both time and money.

Pumpkin plants under heat stress in a polythene tunnel.

Instead of a polythene tunnel or glasshouse you will need to construct a 'mini greenhouse' alongside each plant: a frame of wood or metal approximately 6ft high x 4ft x 4ft (1.80m high x 1.20m x 1.20m). The uprights should be hammered well into the ground to stop it blowing over, and a polythene sheet tacked over the top to protect the young plant from cold winds and late unexpected spring frosts. The roots of the plant will be outside the structure, which will make watering easy and also give them the benefit of any natural rainfall. Two or three weeks before the seedlings are planted out, it is worth covering this planting area with a sheet of polythene to warm the soil and give the young plants a good start.

The American way

Many of the best outdoor growers in America make big mounds of earth, or hillocks, 3–4ft (90–120cm) high, and plant each young pumpkin plant on top of one. As the plant develops, the sap in the main stem rushes downhill to feed the pumpkin lying at the bottom of the mound.

Soil preparation

When preparing the soil, you should add plenty of well rotted farmyard manure, peat or organic material, as this gives a good base and will improve the structure of your soil. You will then need to dig a hole 3ft (90cm) square and 2ft (60cm) deep for each pumpkin plant, and fill it with some of your best growing mixture. Pumpkin roots are very tender and like loose soil full of humus, and in this way the plant's main roots will have plenty of space to grow without obstruction. It may take several years to build up the correct structure for your soil, but excellent results can be obtained the first year, even on virgin soil.

Whether you are growing pumpkins indoors or outdoors, it is esssential never to walk on the soil. If you do, it will compact very quickly, and not only will the roots' progress be stunted, but the liquid feed and water will have great

Pumpkin plant growing on top of a hillock with its stems trailing down the sides.

difficulty in permeating the soil to reach them. If you make walkways during the winter months from old planks or wooden pallets, these should prevent such problems arising. Remember, however, to put some slug pellets and insecticide powder under each one to stop any predators hiding and breeding there.

You must also remember that the more decomposition of materials, including manure, there is, the more nitrogen will be taken from your soil, and this will result in an alteration of your lime levels. I always test my soil a few weeks before planting out, and aim to have a pH level of 6.8, with average nitrogen levels.

Seeds

Obtaining the best seed possible is vital to growing a very large pumpkin; you will not grow a giant from the seeds of a small one. Although pumpkins of all sizes usually produce the same number of seeds – between 350 and 400 – the seeds of a giant will be much bigger. So look for the biggest when buying seeds, and try to find a supplier who has a reputation for growing giants.

Sowing the seeds

We now come to another exciting moment in the pumpkin grower's calendar: sowing the seeds. I always grow three plants for each pumpkin area that I have prepared, and choose

Remember to insert pumpkin seeds the right way up in the compost – the bottom end is pointed and the top is gently rounded, as the first leaves will be.

germination, and a propagator with a lid to create humidity is ideal. The heating element in most propagators is pre-set at around 75° F (24° C), but one with an adjustable thermostat is an advantage. Either way, you will need a temperature of 75° F (24° C) to start with. After three or four days you should see the surface of the soil moving, and the leaves breaking through soon afterwards. As soon as the first two leaves have fully developed, the thermostat should be turned down to 60° F (15° C) and all vents opened or the lid taken off altogether. Too much bottom heat will damage the tender roots at this stage, spoiling your chances of success later on; if you do not have an adjustable thermostat you can lower the temperature by placing several strips of polystyrene or corrugated cardboard under each plant pot to absorb some of the heat.

If you do not have a propagator at all, you can use a warm window sill or warming cables to germinate the seeds. To create the required humidity, the pot should be covered completely with a polythene bag, secured by string or a rubber band, until the first signs of germination when it must be removed.

Unfortunately, poor ventilation encourages the growth of fungus, and these ideal conditions for seedling growth are also ideal conditions for fungus. Use a fungicide spray at the first sign of trouble. Another point to look out for if you are propagating plants on a window sill is that it can get very cold at night. It is wise to move your plants to a warmer position before it gets dark, or when the weather outside becomes very cold.

Transplanting

Provided conditions outside are right, it is time to transplant the young pumpkin plant to its permanent position when it has developed four leaves. However, if plants are to be grown in the open and night time temperatures are dropping below 40° F (4° C), postpone the operation for another week or two. It is better to wait than to have the young leaves frost-damaged, and I have often successfully

the strongest-looking plant before transplanting, eliminating the other two. Pumpkin roots do not like being disturbed, so either start them off in large peat pots, and make additional holes at the bottom with a pencil, or in a 9in (23cm) plant pot. Fill the pots with a peat-based compost mixed with a little Perlite or Vermiculite to keep the compost open and allow the new roots to forage and travel more easily. Then soak the compost thoroughly and dampen the seeds, covering them with a thin layer of seed dressing to prevent them from rotting if they are slow to germinate.

Make a slot with a small stick or pencil about 1½in (4cm) deep in the centre of the compost, and slot the seed in with the pointed end down and the curved end to the top. Cover up the hole and 'hey presto!' the show is on the road.

Bottom heat will be required to assist their

transplanted pumpkin plants 8ft (2.5m) long with ten leaves on each plant. Dig a hole slightly bigger than the plant pot so you can site the plant without too much root disturbance.

Growing on

As it grows, the main stem of the pumpkin plant will need to be covered with a layer of soil to induce small roots to develop beneath each leaf joint. These will help to stabilize the plant and prevent strong winds blowing the tall leaves over. They will also provide extra nutrition for your plant and thus increase your chances of growing a record-breaker. I always prepare a 4in (10cm) groove in the soil across the length of the growing area in the direction in which I want the main stem to travel. As the stem grows along the bottom, I fill the groove in with soil.

It will probably take seven to ten days after transplanting before you notice any significant signs of growth, but from then on, beware: both main stem and laterals (side shoots) may grow 1ft (30cm) each day. If a plant starts to grow in the wrong direction, swing the growing stem around so that it nestles down in its groove.

As the plant grows, the main stem will develop laterals (side shoots). These, like the main stem, should be allowed to travel to the limits of your planned growing area before their growing tips are cut off and the ends covered in soil.

Transplanting a four-leaved pumpkin plant in a specially prepared raised bed.

Pollination

As the main stem continues to develop it will produce male and female flowers; six to eight male flowers will usually form before the first female one appears. You can tell one from the other because the female flower will have a small pumpkin behind it and the male flower will have only a stem (see page 28).

You cannot unfortunately rely with confidence on either bees or a light breeze to pollinate the female flowers for you, and hand-pollination is the only reliable answer. First you must remove a male flower from the plant, being very careful to cut its stalk without disturbing any of the pollen. Then each petal must be removed and the stamen full of pollen inserted into the stigma of the female flower. If after a few days you see a pumpkin the size of a grapefruit, you know you have been successful.

Some years you may find difficulty in pollinating

The pumpkin stem is covered with soil as it grows along the trench; this induces small roots to develop beneath each leaf joint.

The male and female pumpkin flowers are similar, except that the female flower (shown above right) has a small pumpkin growing below it.

pumpkins growing outside as rain or strong winds can destroy the pollen in the male flowers. The best way to get round this is to cover a female flower and a male flower as soon as you see them forming on the plant, using a polythene or even a paper bag tied on with string. When both flowers have opened fully and you have pollinated the female one, cover it up again for a few days and then check to see if you have been successful.

Follow the same procedure with the next few female flowers just in case something goes wrong with your first attempt, but bear in mind that only one pumpkin should eventually be left on each plant. You should also abort any young pumpkins which look misshapen or malformed in any way, as these rarely succeed in growing to a great size.

Feeding
Feeding, of course, is a crucial element in determining the size of a pumpkin. After transplanting the pumpkin plants to their prepared growing areas, I always leave the roots to work for themselves for several weeks before giving them any additional feed. I believe firmly that if a root system is fed too soon, it becomes lazy and will make no effort to establish itself, whereas if you make the roots forage and spread in search of nourishment they will grow large and strong.

This will then be the time to give them some extra food, but it is important not to overdo it – the pumpkin family simply will not stand for it.

If you give pumpkins too much nitrogen they split or become tender; too much potash and the outside skin ripens too soon, stopping the pumpkin's growth prematurely; and too much phosphorus upsets the balance of the whole plant. The best method is 'little and often', and I recommend a liquid feed. This is instantly available as and when the plant needs it, whereas granular or powdered fertilizer may risk being left undissolved under the huge leaves, and will as a result be unable to enter the soil to feed your plant.

Outdoor pumpkins may need to have their pollinated flowers covered with a bag, for protection from wind and rain.

Start with a balanced liquid feed of 20N 20P 20K, and change this six weeks later to 20N 10P 20K, continuing with this formula until harvesting time. It is essential to continue feeding and watering right up to the day of

stigma   stamen

harvesting because although the outside of the pumpkin may have stopped growing, the inside flesh and seeds may be still bulking up, and this can make a tremendous difference to its final weight.

When preparing a liquid feed, always follow the manufacturer's directions exactly, and if the ground is dry, water an hour before you apply it. I foliar-feed pumpkin plants at least once a week, using a ¼-strength balanced feed. I apply this with a sprayer and not a watering can for two reasons: firstly, you can reach much further with a spraying lance and do not need to tread near the plants; secondly, an application with a watering can may sometimes cause too great a weight of water for the leaves to support, and they will sag towards the ground, never to straighten up again.

Foliar feeding should never be carried out in bright sunlight. I always do this job in the morning, especially for plants growing in polythene tunnels. It allows the plants plenty of time to absorb the feed and dry out during the day, preventing the risk of grey mould (botrytis).

Warm water should be used when foliar feeding, to prevent any check to the plants.

Spraying

Although I prefer not to spray my plants with chemicals, in order to have an even chance of success at growing giant pumpkins, a programme for spraying insecticides and fungicides is esssential. And since prevention is better than cure, I always use a systemic spray right from the start, so that plants can build up a resistance to the aphids and diseases that can ruin them. Once pumpkin plants have grown to their full capacity, it is almost impossible to spray under their leaves without causing damage, so a systemic spraying programme carried out every two weeks from the time they are transplanted will be invaluable later in the season.

The insecticide and fungicide may be sprayed together, but when mixing the chemicals do follow the manufacturer's directions exactly; a little extra, or 'one for the pot', could be fatal.

Recording

Try keeping records of planting dates, spraying, feeding, weather conditions, and the measurements of each pumpkin as it grows. It is great fun, and at times amazing, to observe

The easiest form of protection is to spray a systemic insecticide on the undersides of the leaves with a lance.

what happens, good or bad, in hours rather than days. These records can help you as the growing season progresses and will be invaluable when you assess your results and

PUMPKIN HAZARDS

STRESS CRACKS can develop at the back of a pumpkin as it grows over 200lb (90kg). These are caused by the stalk having to lift the weight of the main growing stem off the ground as the pumpkin grows. The point where a stalk joins on to a 500lb (226kg) pumpkin can be as much as 2ft 6in (75cm) above the ground, and this causes a tremendous strain to the back of the pumpkin. If stress cracks do occur it will be only a matter of days or even hours before fruit flies invade the pumpkin and rapidly turn it rotten.

Two things can be done to prevent this. The first is to prevent the main growing stem rooting close to the pumpkin, by removing the leaves from either side of it, and drawing a knife at regular intervals under the stem 3ft (90cm) in each direction. You should start doing this as soon as pollination has been confirmed and the pumpkin is as big as a grapefruit. The other is to support the main growing stem and so take the weight from the stalk. To do this, knock a stake into the ground 1ft (30cm) on either side of the stalk,

and secure a thick piece of cord to the top of each one. These cords can then be used to take the weight of the stem, and can be adjusted as the pumpkin increases in size.

If mice gain access to a pumpkin, they will burrow their way inside it.

RODENTS can be a major problem towards the end of the summer, when mice will come into the polytunnels from the fields and hedges, looking for a cosy home for the winter months. One particular year I noticed some freshly moved earth almost touching the bottom of one of my pumpkins, and discovered that a mouse was building a nest, well lined with fur, underneath the pumpkin.

On another occasion one of my pumpkins stopped growing for no reason when it was about 300lb (136kg) in weight. Once again I discovered a small hole in the ground, and when the pumpkin was moved I could see that a mouse had nibbled its way inside for a grand feast of fresh juicy seeds. This of course was the end of the pumpkin and another lesson learned. I resorted to my old philosophy of prevention being better than

Stakes knocked in on either side of the pumpkin have a length of cord attached to support the main growing stem.

cure: from that day on, I always lay small amounts of mouse bait in dry corners and replenish them when they have been taken.

LOW TEMPERATURES can spoil your chances of breaking records. A pumpkin grows much faster when it is warm, and can stop growing altogether if it gets too cold. Much extra weight can be achieved towards the end of the growing season by covering the pumpkins with blankets in the late afternoon, before the air temperature begins to fall, so that they continue growing throughout the night. If the pumpkin is outside, add a waterproof sheet to prevent the blanket from getting wet if it rains.

Cover your pumpkin with a blanket towards the end of the growing season, from late afternoon onwards.

Estimating Pumpkin and Squash Weights

Largest circumference	Estimated weight	Difference in weight for each 5in (12.5cm) circumference
95in (241.5cm)	204lb (92.5kg)	32lb (14.5kg)
100in (254cm)	236lb (107kg)	33lb (15kg)
105in (266.5cm)	269lb (122kg)	34lb (15.4kg)
110in (279.5cm)	303lb (137.5kg)	34lb (15.4kg)
115in (292cm)	337lb (152.9kg)	35lb (15.8kg)
120in (305cm)	372lb (168.7kg)	35lb (15.8kg)
125in (317.5cm)	407lb (184.6kg)	35lb (15.8kg)
130in (330cm)	442lb (200.5kg)	36lb (16.3kg)
135in (343cm)	478lb (216.8kg)	36lb (16.3kg)
140in (355.5cm)	514lb (233.2kg)	36lb (16.3kg)
145in (368.5cm)	550lb (249.5kg)	37lb (16.8kg)
150in (381cm)	587lb (266.3kg)	37lb (16.8kg)
155in (393.5cm)	624lb (283kg)	37lb (16.8kg)
160in (406.5cm)	661lb (299.8kg)	38lb (17.2kg)
165in (419cm)	699lb (317.1kg)	38lb (17.2kg)

can understand how they were attained.

You can estimate the weight of a pumpkin when it is still growing, and without moving it, by converting the recorded measurements of its circumference. Pumpkins vary in shape – some are taller and others longer – but you will be surprised with the accuracy of the chart above. Using a length of string or cord, which will not damage or scratch a tender young pumpkin as a tape measure might do, measure the circumference of the pumpkin from one side of the stalk, around its widest part, and back to the other side of the stalk. You must keep the string parallel with the ground and measure the pumpkin in exactly the same place each time you do it. Then measure the string and use the chart above to arrive at the pumpkin's estimated weight.

Harvesting

Once you are sure that your pumpkins have stopped growing, inside and outside, you must keep a keen watch on the weather. Try to delay

pumpkin pie

12oz (350g) cooked pumpkin
6oz (175g) caster sugar
1 teaspoon ground cinnamon
1/4 teaspoon nutmeg
1/2 teaspoon ground ginger
1/2 teaspoon salt
1 tablespoon plain flour
2 eggs
1/2 pint (300ml) evaporated milk
9in (23cm) unbaked pie shell

1. Heat oven to 425°F, 220°C, Gas mark 7.
2. Combine all ingredients and mix well.
Pour into the unbaked pie shell and bake for
15 minutes until the filling is quite firm.
3. Serve warm or cold with fresh cream,
brandy cream or Greek yoghurt.

pumpkin wine

6lb (2.5kg) pumpkin, peeled and chopped
1lb (450g) wheat
2 oranges
2 lemons
3lb (1.5kg) sugar
1lb (450g) raisins
1/2- 3/4 oz (15-20g) ginger
1oz (25g) yeast
1 gallon (4.5 litres) boiling water

1. Place the chopped pumpkin in a 1 1/2 gallon
(6.5 litre) plastic bucket.
2. Chop the raisins, lemons and oranges, and
add them to the pumpkin with the ginger and
wheat, and lastly add the sugar.
3. Pour on the boiling water and, when cool,
add the yeast, creamed with a little liquid.
4. Stir once a day for ten days, then strain off
into a fermentation jar.
NB. Keep covered because of
tiny flies.

pumpkin cookies

8oz (225g) sugar
4oz (115g) margarine
1 small egg
8oz (225g) pumpkin
8oz (225g) flour
6oz (175g) mixed dried fruit
2 teaspoons cinnamon
1 teaspoon vanilla essence
1 teaspoon each baking powder and
bicarbonate of soda
pinch of salt

1. Heat oven to 375°F, 190°C, Gas mark 5.
2. Mix ingredients well together, and drop
spoonfuls on a greased baking tray. Bake for
8- 10 minutes.
3. These are good as they are, or may be iced
if there are sweet teeth in the family.

pumpkin chutney

2lb (900g) pumpkin, peeled,
cored and seeded
1lb (450g) tomatoes, skinned and chopped
1lb (450g) onions, skinned and chopped
1 clove garlic, crushed (optional)
2oz (50g) sultanas
1 1/2 lb (750g) soft brown sugar
1 pint (600ml) white wine vinegar
1 teaspoon ground allspice
1 tablespoon salt
1 teaspoon black pepper

1. Cut the pumpkin flesh into 1/2 in (1.25cm)
cubes and place all ingredients in a
preserving pan.
2. Bring to the boil and simmer gently for
about one hour, stirring occasionally,
especially towards the end of the cooking
time, until no excess liquid remains and the
mixture is thick.

3. Spoon the chutney into preheated jars and cover immediately with airtight and vinegar-proof tops.
Makes about 5lb (2.25kg).

pumpkin and orange dessert

2lb (900g) pumpkin flesh
6oz (175g) sugar
¼ pint (150ml) orange juice
3oz (75g) ground walnuts, almonds or hazelnuts, or mixed chopped nuts
To serve: whipped cream or ice cream

1. Cut pumpkin flesh into 1in (2.5cm) slices, put in pan with layers of sugar, and add orange juice.
2. Cover and cook over medium heat until tender, then cool in the pan.
3. Remove to a dish and decorate with nuts. Serve with cream or ice cream.

pumpkin and cheese soup

1 pint (600ml) stock or water
10-12oz (275-330g) sliced pumpkin
4oz (115g) lentils
seasoning
2-3oz (50-75g) grated cheese

1. Put stock or water in pan and add pumpkin, lentils and seasoning. Cook for 45 minutes or until tender.
2. Push through a colander, then return to the pan, add cheese and reheat, but do not boil. Serve hot. with croutons.

harvesting for as long as possible, but pumpkins will not stand a frost or very cold winds, so if conditions deteriorate you must 'cut and run'; they will lose a little weight after being harvested, but it is better to forfeit this than lose your pumpkins altogether.

When the pumpkin has been detached from the plant, the rest of the plant must be cleared away before the 'heavy gang' is brought in to remove the pumpkin.

For this mammoth task, I use a canvas sheet measuring 8ft x 4ft (2.5m x 1.2m). I roll the pumpkin half over one way, then fold the strip of canvas in half lengthwise and arrange it underneath before rolling the pumpkin back on to the canvas and a little way further. The fold can then be unfolded, and the pumpkin rolled back to rest in the centre of the canvas. It is then ready, with the help of many willing hands, to be lifted on its triumphant way. Great care must be taken not to scratch or mark it for, however huge in size, pumpkins are still very tender and easily damaged.

If you intend to store your pumpkin in a shed or garage, stand it on a wooden pallet or on six thicknesses of cardboard, cover it with a blanket, and surround it with several containers of mouse poison. The ideal storage temperature for pumpkins is 60˚F (15˚C).

Cutting the stalk to harvest the pumpkin – always a sad moment for me.

tomatoes

Hundreds of tomato varieties are grown throughout the world, with colours ranging from yellow to dark red, skins varying from thick to thin, tastes ranging from bitter to very sweet, and sizes from ½ in (1.25 cm) to 7in (18cm) across.

In many countries tomatoes are grown in the open fields all year round; in other colder climates they are produced in heated glasshouses for a six or seven month season at far higher cost. Tomatoes are often shipped thousands of miles to fulfil the constant demand of countries which have a short growing season.

Although a tomato is actually a fruit, for horticultural judging purposes it is classified as a vegetable. The interest in growing big tomatoes increases year after year, and seed of dozens of giant varieties can now be purchased from garden centres, stores and from mail order catalogues. The ones I grow, which usually measure 7–8in (18–20cm), weigh on average 3lb (1.35kg) each, are very juicy and in fact taste superb.

I will never forget the first time I grew a giant tomato. It weighed in at just over 2lb (900g), and when the news leaked out about my 'huge red monster' I must have had a visit from almost every gardener in the neighbourhood.

The following year I provided seeds for everyone to try, and the district was renamed 'the land of the giant tomatoes'. Jokes abounded: 'You don't get many of those for a pound'; or, 'Could you sell me a pound of tomatoes?' to which the reply was, 'I'm not cutting one up for you or anyone'.

Planning ahead

There are two different types of tomato plants: indeterminate, which are the bush type, and determinate, which

Bush tomatoes (right) are usually good producers, but I prefer to grow determinate varieties (far right) to produce my giants; this type is also easier to train.

need to be supported and secured to canes or a trellis. The second type is easier to train and is the one described throughout this chapter.

There are also three different methods of cultivation: raised beds, peat-based growing bags, and in open ground. Whichever method you decide to use, the foliage from each plant will need an area of at least 3ft (90cm) square, with an 18in (45cm) walkway between each row. The timescale from sowing seed to harvesting the tomatoes ranges from fourteen to twenty-four weeks.

In this chapter I will be describing how to grow giant tomatoes in a glasshouse, but the same growing techniques apply if you are able to grow them outside in the open garden. Just choose a site facing south, and provide some kind of wind protection.

A plastic drum, cut in half, makes an excellent raised bed in which to grow a single tomato plant.

Soil preparation

Tomato plants are notorious for transmitting diseases and viruses into the soil. To avoid this some gardeners change the soil in their glasshouses every few years. This is very hard work, and I have not changed my soil for the past twenty years. However, at the end of each growing season, I always dig up the roots of my tomato plants intact, and relegate the entire plant and any loose leaves and debris to a garden fire or the dustbin, not the compost heap. I then spray the inside of the glasshouse with a disinfectant liquid, and drench the ground with a soil sterilizer. I repeat the soil drench in mid-winter and then leave it alone until transplanting time in the spring.

Soil for growing tomato plants should be deeply dug and have plenty of humus incorporated into its structure. I do not recommend the use of farmyard manure in a glasshouse, but if your soil is of a clay type you can improve its structure by digging in some peat or sterilized compost.

The pH level is not critical for growing tomatoes, but I usually test my soil towards the end of winter, and aim for a 6.6 reading.

Growing bags

Peat-based growing bags are used by many gardeners to grow tomatoes both on soil in glasshouses and on concrete surfaces. I recommend this method where the bags are sited on soil, but I believe it is a mistake to place growing bags on hard surfaces – either indoors or out. A growing bag must have holes or slits in the bottom, as a plant pot has, to prevent the compost becoming waterlogged and turning into a swamp. Fresh water flowing to the roots will provide the plant with essential oxygen, but it is important that surplus water can drain away. If a growing bag is placed on top of freshly cultivated soil, some of the tomato's roots will also grow through the holes and establish themselves in the soil. These will not only provide your plants with extra nutrition but will keep them alive on a very hot day if the contents of the growing bag dry out, whereas

Tomato plants to be grown in open ground should be potted on individually into 5in (12cm) pots once the seedlings have four to six leaves.

Sowing the seeds

Timing is very important if you require a giant tomato for a special event or a competitive show. The third or fourth truss on a tomato plant will usually produce the biggest tomatoes, and to have a fully developed tomato on these trusses by early autumn, the seed should be sown in mid-summer. (This timing can, of course, be adjusted either way.) The seeds should be sown ¼in (6mm) deep in a tray of peat-based compost, and watered thoroughly. The tray should then be placed on the glasshouse bench or an indoor window sill, and covered with a pane of glass or a polythene bag to create humidity. If the night time temperature falls below 40° F (4° C) use a propagator with a bottom heat of 60–75° F (15–24° C). Germination should take five or six days, and as soon as this occurs the seedlings should be potted on into 3in (7cm) pots containing the same type of compost, and grown on in full daylight.

Always sow enough seeds to produce a surplus of young plants. This will enable you to select the strongest ones for transplanting when the time comes.

Transplanting

When your young tomato plants have developed four to six leaves, the roots should have started to grow through the bottom of their pots.

A tomato weighing 7lb 12oz (3.51kg) was grown in 1986 by Mr Gordon Graham in Edmond, Oklahoma, U.S.A.

If you are using raised beds or peat growing bags, your plants can now be set into their permanent growing positions and tied to their supporting canes as they grow. Those that are to be grown in the ground should be potted on into 5in (12cm) pots of compost, with a thin 18in (45cm) cane inserted into the compost to support the plants as they grow. Once your tomato plants have reached the top of the

plants in bags on top of concrete will perish. If your budget allows, you could of course use a drip feed or automatic watering system to prevent this happening.

Raised beds

I prefer the raised bed system for my giant tomatoes. The beds can be made from a strong wooden box, or half of a plastic 45 gallon (200 litre) drum, with the top and bottom removed. The main purpose of raised beds is for them to contain your best growing mixture, so that the plant's roots can develop into a very strong system even before reaching the cultivated soil underneath.

Seeds

Tomato seeds are some of the toughest in the horticultural world. They can pass through the human body without being destroyed by body acid, and they will store for at least ten years. It is very important to purchase the correct variety of giant tomato seeds if you are trying to break records, and I recommend an open-pollinated variety, not an F1 hybrid. They may be expensive, but if they are from good stock you will be able to save the seeds from the first season's biggest tomato to use in future years.

In raised beds, tomato plants can be transplanted straight to their permanent positions and attached to their support canes as they grow.

Burying the main stem of a tomato plant will encourage extra roots to develop from it. Lay the stem in a small trench 3in (7cm) deep and 12in (30cm) long.

canes, they will be ready to transfer to their permanent growing position.

You should make a small trench 3in (7cm) deep and 12in (30cm) long, with a strong supporting cane inserted at one end of it. The tomato plant should then be carefully taken from its pot and the lower leaves removed. Lay the stem in the trench and cover it with soil, leaving about four full leaves and the growing tip above the soil, alongside the cane. The reason for burying some of the stem in the ground is so that hundreds of extra roots will develop along it, giving your plant extra vigour. Your tomato should be grown on in the same way as those in raised beds or growing bags.

Growing on

All laterals (side shoots) should be removed as soon as they appear, and the main stem of the

plant should be secured to the supporting cane every 6in (15cm) as it grows. As each truss develops small tomatoes, these should be thinned out, leaving just the strongest one to grow on each truss. If you have enough headroom, you could allow your plant to form six or seven trusses before cutting off the growing tip.

Pollination

Tomato plants pollinate very easily, whether under glass or outside in the garden. Midday is supposed to be the optimum time for pollination, but at that time of day I, like others, am usually at work. With my tomato plants grown under glass, I therefore make a habit of tapping the tomatoes' supporting canes every time I walk past them, to knock the pollen into the air and make it spread from flower to flower. This method has always given me a 99 per cent success rate. Bees and insects will normally pollinate plants growing outside.

Feeding

I do not feed tomato plants growing in soil or raised beds until I am sure that the first truss has been pollinated successfully. The plant's roots should be fully developed by this time, and ready and waiting for their first treat. Plants in growing bags will need feeding much sooner, as the fertilizers in most bags will be exhausted after two or three weeks.

Commercial tomato feeds, whether liquid, soluble or granular, will all have a high potash level which is designed to shorten the plant's lifespan and encourage the fruit to ripen off more quickly. This, however, is just what you do not want to happen if you are trying to grow 'monsters'. You want plants to continue growing for as long as possible, and to achieve this a low potash formula is needed. I use a compound formula of 15N 5P 15K up until two weeks before harvest time, and then change to 5N 5P 15K to ripen them off. You are likely to do more harm than good unless you follow the manufacturer's instructions exactly when mixing feeds, and it is important not to feed more often than recommended. However, a ¼ strength foliar feed twice a week is an acceptable addition.

When a tomato plant has grown to a height of 4ft (1.2m) and has developed three or four trusses of tomatoes, it can consume 5–6 gallons

---

TOMATO HAZARDS

SPLITTING is usually caused by allowing the soil or growing mixture to dry out and then watering heavily. The plant will take up too much liquid too quickly, resulting in some of the tomatoes splitting their skins.

WHITEFLY is the most common of all tomato pests. Both the adult and larvae will suck sap from the leaves which will then become pale and curled. Whitefly can breed four days after hatching out, so if you develop an infestation, spray with an aphid insecticide at least four times at three-day intervals.

BLOSSOM END ROT is indicated by dark brown patches forming in the centre of a tomato. There are two main causes: the first is malnutrition; if a plant lacks water or nutrients it will feed on the tomatoes themselves. The second is when there is a noticeable difference between day and night time temperatures.

TRUSS STEM BENDING will tend to happen when a tomato exceeds 1lb (450g) in weight, unless the plant is supported from above by string or cord fastened to the roof of the glasshouse or to the supporting cane.

LEAF ROLL is usually caused by over-watering. Unfortunately, this is an occupational hazard when growing giants, but although the plants may not look too healthy, they seem to cope quite well.

YELLOW PATCHES ON THE LEAVES mean that there is a magnesium deficiency in your growing mixture or soil. It can be rectified by adding ¼ oz (5g) of epsom salts per gallon (5 litres) of liquid feed once a month.

RED SPIDER MITE can also be a problem, and an infestation can be identified by a fine silky web covering the leaves, which may appear bleached or speckled. The tiny mites can be found on the undersides of leaves and will need a strong insecticide to eliminate them. However, they hate moist, damp conditions, so foliar feeding should help to deter them.

Each truss should be thinned out at an early stage, leaving the strongest tomato to grow on each truss. There should be between four and seven trusses on each plant.

(22–27 litres) of liquid a week. (I discovered this during trials, using an isolated capillary system.) As 80 per cent of the liquid applied to plants growing in the ground will very quickly leach down, out of reach of the plant's roots, you can imagine the amount of water that is needed for a plant to be able to collect 5 gallons (22 litres). However, it is far better to water little but often, rather than waterlog the ground every few days.

To harvest your tomatoes, use scissors or a sharp knife to cut the stalk, leaving no more than 1in (2.5cm) attached to the tomato.

Spraying

A spraying programme is essential when cultivating tomatoes, but I do not recommend using systemic chemicals. A thorough application of a fungicide spray every two weeks throughout the season should keep grey mould (botrytis) at bay, and regular spraying with insecticide should keep green, black and white aphids under control.

Harvesting

Tomatoes can be harvested at any time of the year, but if your giant specimen has developed too early for a particular show or special event, you can harvest it as soon as its green colour turns to yellow. The tomato will then keep for at least another three weeks in a refrigerator set at a medium temperature.

If, on the other hand, your giant is slow to develop and needs pushing on, apply a high potash feed two weeks before harvesting. To qualify for the Guinness Book of Records, a tomato must be in a sound condition and have a maximum stalk length of 1in (2.5cm) at time of weighing. It can be any colour.

tomato sauce

4lb (1.8kg) ripe tomatoes, peeled and
chopped
4 tablespoons olive or vegetable oil
1 level tablespoon cayenne pepper
$\frac{1}{4}$ level teaspoon paprika pepper
4oz (115g) sugar
$\frac{1}{2}$ pint (300ml) vinegar

1. Place the chopped tomatoes with
the oil in a pan over a low heat to begin
with; gradually increase the heat and boil to
a thick pulp, stirring from time to time.
2. Rub the pulp through a sieve.
Add seasoning, sugar and vinegar
and return to the pan.
3. Continue boiling and stirring until the
sauce is of a thick, creamy consistency.
4. Pour into clean, hot bottles and
cork at once.

tomato soup

1oz (25g) margarine
1 small carrot, peeled and diced
2 celery stalks, washed and diced
1 onion, peeled and chopped
1 giant tomato, quartered
1 bouquet garni
salt and pepper
1 teaspoon sugar
2 cloves
1 pint (600ml) stock
1oz (25g) flour
2 tablespoons milk
chopped parsley to garnish

1. Melt the margarine in a saucepan and fry
the carrot, celery and onion until they are
softened.

2. Add the tomato, seasonings, sugar, cloves
and stock. Bring to the boil, then cover and
simmer for 20 minutes or until the
vegetables are tender.
3. Put the soup through a sieve, then return
to the pan.
4. Dissolve the flour in the milk until it is of
a smooth consistency, then add to the soup;
simmer for another 15 minutes.
5. Serve hot, sprinkled with chopped parsley.

stuffed giant tomato

1 giant tomato weighing about 2lb (900g)
4 tablespoons mayonnaise
8oz (225g) cream cheese
2 tablespoons chopped chives
salt
pinch cayenne pepper
cucumber slice or parsley to garnish

1. Cut off the top of the tomato and carefully
scoop out the pulp and the seeds with a
teaspoon.
2. Mix the mayonnaise with the softened
cream cheese, then add the tomato pulp and
mix well.
3. Add the chopped chives, salt and cayenne
pepper to taste and mix well.
4. Sppon this mixture back into the tomato
and garnish with a slice of cucumber or a
sprig of parsley.

chapter four

carrots for weight

The carrot is a hardy biennial native of Europe and has long been cultivated in lands bordering the Eastern Mediterranean. It was introduced into England in about 1600, and is now grown worldwide in huge quantities.

The roots of wild carrots are white or pale yellow in colour, but cultivated varieties range from red to orange. They come in all shapes and sizes, from the thick-rooted stump variety, to the very long and slender types which I describe in the last chapter. A carrot root contains about 4½ per cent sugar, is high in vitamins, low in calories, and is therefore an ideal subject for many diets. Carrots are easy to preserve: they can be frozen, canned or stored in dry sand for use throughout the year.

Planning ahead

Growing giant carrots is easy and economical – since they do not require artificial heat and thrive on fresh air, they should always be grown in the open garden. They take thirty-six to forty weeks from sowing the seed to harvesting.

Carrot seeds can be sown directly into the soil, which should be deeply cultivated and contain a high content of humus or organic material, giving a pH of 6.7. I grow mine in 2ft 6in (75cm) high raised beds with a growing mixture of one-third sand, one-third soil and one-third peat. These ideal conditions allow the carrot roots to travel through a good depth of growing mixture before even reaching the cultivated garden soil. The soil or growing mixture should be covered with a sheet of polythene a week before the late winter sowing, to raise the surface temperature a little and ensure successful germination.

Seeds

There are dozens of different varieties of carrot seeds on sale throughout the world, but I advise a heavy-shouldered variety, of intermediate length. The seeds will keep for at least five years if stored in an airtight tin at room temperature, so if you have any surplus when your seed-sowing programme has been completed, you can safely keep them for the next season.

Once the seedlings are about 5in (12cm) high, tap a group out of the pot and break the compost apart to find the strongest root in each group.

Select the strongest looking seedling in each group and cut about 1in (2.5cm) off the tip of the root before inserting it in a planting hole in the ground.

Six carrot seeds should be sown in each growing position, ¼ in (6mm) deep and 18in (45cm) apart in both directions. They should be covered with a thin layer of fine soil or sand and watered lightly. I always mark each sowing position with a small stick so as to avoid disturbing the seeds with later sowings. As soon as the late winter sowing has been completed, the ground should once again be covered with the polythene sheet, but this should be removed at the first sign of germination.

Growing on

First, it is necessary to say a word about how to maximize the weight of a carrot, which is to produce as many forks as possible. When growing carrots for exhibition or household use, it is annoying when you find that a root has forked. The carrot will be useless for the show bench, and difficult to prepare for cooking. However, this is exactly what is required when you are growing giant carrots for weight. The greater number of forks a carrot has, the heavier it should weigh.

Sometimes a carrot's root will fork naturally, if the soil or growing mixture is too rich or contains fresh farmyard manure, for example, or if the carrot meets some sort of obstruction such as a stone.

But the method I have devised to make my giant carrot roots fork is as follows: I dig up all the seedlings in each growing position when the foliage has grown to a height of 5in (12cm), and carefully shake the soil from the roots. I then select the strongest-looking plant in each group and cut off the bottom 1in (2.5cm) of the root. This will stop the main root from growing

Sowing the seeds

Carrots have a very long growing season, and if weather conditions are favourable I make the first of three seed sowings directly into the ground in late winter, a second in early spring, and a final one in mid-spring. The reason for this is that some years the early sowings will fail completely, usually because cold damp soil causes the seeds to rot. However, the earlier sowings are worth doing, because the sooner successful germination can be achieved, the more chance you have of growing a record-breaker.

CARROT HAZARDS

WOODLICE love a feast of newly germinated carrot seedlings, and you may be unaware of their presence until you find that your once healthy carrot seedlings have disappeared overnight. To keep such predators away from your tender seedlings, sprinkle insecticide powder or granules on to the soil or growing mixture a week after the seeds have been sown. Once the plants have developed four leaves they must lose some of their taste, for the woodlice then seem to steer clear of them.

CARROT ROOT FLY is another deadly enemy of the carrot. The fly lays its eggs alongside the root, and these eventually hatch into white maggots ¼ in (6mm) long, which bore into the carrot and will eventually cause rotting along its whole length. Since the carrot root fly travels just above ground level, plants growing in raised beds are usually safe from this pest, but it is wise to apply insecticide powder or granules to the whole growing area, a week after the seeds have been sown, and this should be repeated each time the plants are weeded or disturbed.

SLUGS AND SNAILS may cause problems towards the end of the growing season by nibbling chunks from the shoulder of the developed carrot at soil level. If you sprinkle a few long-lasting mini slug pellets

around each carrot, you should find that this is sufficient to prevent these pests from operating.

SPLITTING is usually caused by allowing the growing mixture or soil to dry out and then drenching it. The sudden uptake of liquid will be too great for the plant to handle, and the carrot will split from top to bottom. Sometimes the crack will heal over, but more often than not the carrot will then begin to rot.

If the soil around your plant has been allowed to dry out, therefore, do not flood it with water, but apply a little every two hours until the soil has returned to its normal condition.

For the same reason, when cleaning a carrot for display purposes, do not suddenly submerge it in water as this treatment might cause it to split.

Your aim should be to harvest a multiforked carrot root.

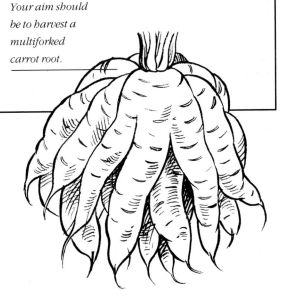

any further and will induce the plant to form three or four additional ones from the base of the foliage.

You must then make a deep hole in the ground with a cane, carefully transplant your mutilated carrot into it, and water it gently every day until the carrot plant has fully recovered from its ordeal.

Feeding

However strong and healthy your carrot plants appear after their transplanting, you should not give them any additional feed until mid-summer. This will allow time for their roots to grow long in search of food; then some extra nutrients are needed to make them grow thick and heavy.

From now on until harvesting, a balanced liquid feed (20N 20P 20K) should be applied once a week in the late evening. If the soil or growing mixture surrounding the carrot plants is dry, water the soil approximately an hour before applying the liquid feed.

A carrot weighing 15lb 7oz (7.03kg) was grown in 1978 by Mr I. Scott in Nelson, New Zealand.

Harvesting

When you harvest a giant carrot it is crucial not to break any of the small roots from the main

It is most important to keep the soil moist, so water your carrots regularly. If the soil is allowed to dry out, there is a risk that the carrots will split.

body, because every ½oz (15g) will count at the weigh-in; a small piece of root could make the difference between winning or losing, or even breaking that elusive record.

I find the safest way is to remove most of the surrounding soil with my fingers, before easing the carrot carefully from the ground by its foliage. I then clean the carrot by holding it up in the air by the foliage and hosing it down with a medium pressure of water. To prevent a carrot losing weight after being harvested, only remove the foliage at the last minute before it is weighed.

To qualify for entry into the record books, a carrot should be free from dirt, sticks, stones or any other foreign matter. The foliage should be cut off as close to the shoulder as possible, and it should be in a sound condition.

carrot cake

6oz (175g) butter
6oz (175g) soft brown sugar
2 eggs, well beaten
8oz (225g) plain flour
½ teaspoon baking powder
1½ teaspoons bicarbonate of soda
¼ teaspoon ground cinnamon
¼ teaspoon ground nutmeg
½ teaspoon salt
8oz (225g) carrot, peeled and grated
3oz (75g) raisins
2oz (50g) walnuts, finely chopped
¼ teaspoon cardamom seeds, crushed
icing sugar for dredging

1. Cream the butter and sugar together until they are light and fluffy. Add the eggs a little at a time, beating well, and add a teaspoon of flour with each addition.
2. Sieve together the remaining flour in a large bowl with the bicarbonate of soda, baking powder, cinnamon, nutmeg and salt.
3. Carefully fold the flour into the butter and egg mixture. Add the carrots, raisins, nuts and cardamom seeds.
4. Lightly grease a 10in (25cm) cake tin and bake in a preheated oven at 350°F, 180°C Gas mark 4, for 45-50 minutes.
5. Dredge with icing sugar before serving.

fried carrots

1 giant carrot weighing about 2lb (1kg)
2 tablespoons flour
salt and pepper
4 tablespoons olive oil
1 pint (600ml) natural yoghurt
2 level tablespoons chopped mint _or_
2 teaspoons caraway seeds, to garnish

1. Peel or scrape the carrot, then cut it into slices approximately ¼in (6mm) thick.
2. Bring a pan of salted water to the boil and cook the carrots for about 10 minutes or until tender.
3. Drain well, then spread the carrots on kitchen paper to dry. Toss the slices in the seasoned flour, shaking off any surplus.
4. Heat the oil in a heavy-based pan and fry the carrots over moderate heat until golden brown. Season to taste.
5. Put the yoghurt in a separate pan over a low heat and let it warm through gently.
6. Serve with the yoghurt topping poured over the top and sprinkle with garnish.

carrot and potato crunch

1 giant carrot, weighing about 2lb (1kg), peeled and chopped
2lb (1kg) potatoes, peeled and chopped
2 tablespoons oil
1 large onion, peeled and sliced
1 clove garlic, crushed
1 pint (600ml) cheese sauce
3oz (75g) flaked almonds
4oz (115g) mature Cheddar cheese, grated
chopped parsley, to garnish

1. Cook the carrot and potatoes in boiling salted water for about 10 minutes.
2. Drain and place in an ovenproof dish.
3. Heat the oil in a frying pan and fry the onion and garlic, until softened. Mix with the carrot and potatoes.
4. Pour over the cheese sauce. Combine almonds and grated cheese: sprinkle on top.
5. Bake in a preheated oven at 400°F, 200°C, Gas mark 6, for 40-45 minutes or until the top is golden brown.
Garnish with parsley to serve.

cabbages

Cabbages are one of the easiest vegetables to grow, and it is possible to grow varieties that will produce different shapes, sizes and colours all year round.

Cabbages are high in vitamins, including iron, and can be pickled, boiled, baked, braised or stuffed with minced meat and herbs. They can also be used in soups or casseroles or eaten raw with salads.

Growing a giant cabbage is an experience not to be missed. You will hardly be able to believe your eyes when you grow one measuring over 3ft (90cm) high and 6ft (1.8m) across. You will only be able to hazard a guess at its weight.

People will say, 'What on earth do you want with a cabbage that size?' or 'What are you going to do with it when you have harvested it?' Do not be deterred. Once my giants have been weighed and measured I usually give them to a nearby hospital, and the kitchen staff are always delighted to have them.

There are two main types of cabbage: green and red. A red cabbage of exactly the same outside measurements as a green one will prove far heavier. The giant green cabbage strain that I first developed had massive outside leaves and used to grow to an average weight of 50lb (22kg). In 1988 I cross-pollinated one with a large red one and the following year I broke the world record with a specimen measuring 6ft x 8ft (1.8m x 2.5m) and weighing 124lb (56kg). It was impossible to get it through my garden gate; we had to use a crane to lift it over the fence and load it on to a lorry to be transported to the UK Giant Vegetable Championships. It was a great event, and everyone involved in the operation enjoyed it to the full.

Some of my friends began by being a little sceptical about the excitement of growing 'the big one', so one spring I offered them some of my young

A cabbage weighing 124lb (56kg) was grown by Bernard Lavery in Llanharry, South Wales.

Corporal Isabel Douce is dwarfed by two giant cabbages exhibited at an airforce horticultural show in 1949.

This young cabbage has been supported using wooden stakes and wire netting. The seedling was transplanted into a hole cut in the middle of the netting and can now be watered and fed easily.

cabbage plants to grow in their gardens. They were soon converted. At the end of that season I was inundated with enthusiastic reports of the challenge and the pleasure they had experienced in growing their giant specimens, and with orders for more plants for the coming season.

Planning ahead

There are two ways of growing cabbages, with seed being sown either in the autumn or in the spring. Nature's way is in the autumn, when the seed falls from the plants to the ground, but this method may have a detrimental effect on your plants if they are subjected to the experience of a severely cold winter. The check that the cabbages will suffer may not be apparent at the time but it will affect them later in the year, causing them to come to fruition before reaching their full potential.

The timescale from sowing the seeds to

harvesting your cabbages ranges from thirty-five to forty-five weeks.

Soil preparation

Cabbages thrive on rich retentive soil, deeply cultivated and well manured. They like an open situation free from the shade of buildings or trees. Fresh manure should only be used for spring-grown plants, and this should be dug into the ground in the autumn and left to decompose all through the winter.

Like all brassicas, cabbages prefer a high lime content in the soil; a pH of 7–7.5 will be ideal. If like myself you adopt a four-year crop rotation programme (see page 18), cabbages should always be grown in the soil which has most recently had an application of lime. They should be moved to a new limed patch every year, and only in the fifth year allowed back to the same soil. A general purpose fertilizer should be raked into the top 1in (2.5cm) of the soil, two weeks before transplanting.

A giant cabbage will usually need at least ten times more space to grow in than an ordinary one, and I recommend that each seedling be transplanted into the centre of a 6ft (1.8m) square area of ground.

Supporting the leaves

One of the major problems that I encountered in my early days of growing giant cabbages was that they were very difficult to water properly once they had grown quite big. The huge outside leaves rested heavily on the ground, and the once cultivated soil underneath them would compress and dry out as hard as concrete.

After trying various solutions, I finally came up with an answer. Before transplanting my cabbage seedlings I now hammer three short stakes approximately 18in (45cm) long into the ground at 2ft (60cm) intervals on two opposite sides of my growing area. I leave about 10in (25cm) above the ground, and staple a length of pig or chicken wire netting to the top, making sure that the netting is drawn tight before I staple it into its final position. When this operation has been completed, I cut out a 1ft (30cm) square section in the centre, which is where the giant cabbage seedling will go. As the plant grows, the outside leaves must be checked every few days to make sure that they are resting freely above the wire netting.

I now have ready access to the soil underneath the cabbage, so that the roots can be thoroughly watered and the bottom leaves sprayed to prevent disease and damage from garden pests.

Seeds

It is important to have the correct variety of seeds if you intend to grow a huge cabbage, and you should select a variety which is purported to have the genetic capabilities to produce large specimens.

Cabbages, like most brassicas, take two years to produce seeds; a two-year-old cabbage plant should yield over 200,000 seeds. If you decide to grow one for seed, the harvested seeds should be stored at room temperature in an airtight container, when they should keep for four to five years. However, if a plant goes to seed in its first year, it is generally referred to as a 'bolter', and seeds from these plants will be unstable and should be discarded.

Sowing the seeds

The greatest challenge Mother Nature presents to a gardener is the weather, and varying conditions will greatly affect the production of your giant cabbages. Cabbages thrive in a mild winter and may suffer a check in a severe one. They love rainy days but hate very high temperatures or direct, blistering sunshine. To meet this challenge, I always sow some seed in the early autumn and the remainder in late winter. These are all intended for an early autumn harvest, but during some years the earlier-sown cabbages will mature in late summer.

Autumn sowing I usually make my autumn sowing early this season. Although I will grow only five plants on through the winter, I sow at least fifty seeds ¼in (6mm) deep in a small tray of thoroughly watered peat-based compost. The tray then goes into an electric propagator with a heat setting of 65° F (18° C). The seeds should germinate in seven to eight days, and I then pot the seedlings on into individual 3in (7cm) plant pots.

Spring sowing The young cabbage seedlings will soon need planting out into their permanent positions in the garden, and if you are restricted for space in your garden in winter, it is better to sow the seeds in spring. Sow them at the end of winter if you have a heated

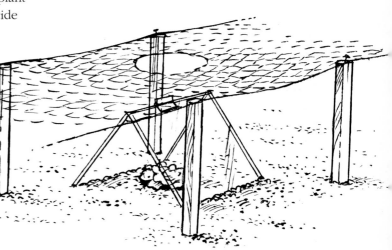

A newly transplanted cabbage seedling is given extra protection under glass below the netting enclosure.

CABBAGE HAZARDS

CLUB ROOT (Fingers and Toes) is a common disease to affect cabbages. It can be transmitted by foot, as well as by cats, dogs and, most commonly of all, birds. It is identified by the presence of large gall-like growths at the roots; in severe cases the whole root system will look like a club foot. It will stunt a plant and make it wilt in hot weather. There is no cure for infected plants, and they should be relegated to the dustbin. Chemical products are available for treating infected soil to prevent the trouble spreading, but even after treatment it is not advisable to grow any kind of brassica in the same soil for at least five years.

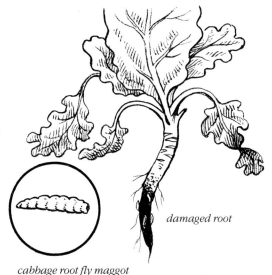

damaged root

cabbage root fly maggot

A plant with swollen roots like this should be removed from the ground intact.

CABBAGE ROOT FLY can attack two or three times during the growing season. The first brood of flies will appear in mid- or late spring, the second in mid-summer, and a third sometimes in late summer. The flies are ash grey in colour and are similar to a house fly. They deposit their tiny white eggs alongside the stem of a cabbage, just below the surface of the soil, and hatch out into small maggots which will gnaw through the whole root system and sometimes even devour part of the stem in a very short space of time. The first visible sign of trouble will be when some of the cabbage leaves turn blue, or the plant wilts in hot weather. There is little chance of saving infected plants, and the best procedure is to dig them up, place both the plant and the soil around the roots in a plastic bag, and deposit the whole lot in the dustbin. If the root has already been devoured, search the surrounding soil for any remaining maggots before they travel to the next plant.

Once again, prevention is better than cure, and I always sprinkle a little insecticide powder on to the soil at the foot of each cabbage when I transplant it, and again when the manufacturer's instructions advise. The pungent smell of the powder will usually be enough to deter the dreaded fly.

CATERPILLARS most commonly found on brassicas are those of the large garden white or cabbage butterfly. These have two broods a year, one in early summer and the other in late summer when the greatest damage occurs. The butterflies lay small yellow eggs in clusters of 50 to 100 on or under the leaves, and these must be removed within seven days, before they hatch out. The clusters of eggs are easily missed, even after a thorough search, and if this happens, caterpillars will soon be evident. At first, small holes will appear in the leaves, and if the caterpillars are not removed by hand or destroyed with an insecticide spray they will strip the leaves down to the ribs, leaving them looking like skeletons.

MEALY BUG is an aphid similar to greenfly, but is much more destructive to a cabbage plant. It causes the leaves to curl and blister and this will dramatically restrict the plant's growth. Apply a suitable insecticide spray to the plants at the first signs of damage.

CABBAGE WHITE FLY can produce some five generations in a year. Eggs will be laid in circles under the cabbage leaves, in a small wax patch. They look like small splashes of whitewash and are commonly called 'scales'.

Whitefly will devastate cabbage plants if left unchecked, and by the end of the season the plants will be covered with a dirty dark tar-like residue. To eliminate the whitefly, apply a spray of suitable insecticide to the whole plant, and to the soil underneath, every three days for a twelve-day period.

SLUGS AND SNAILS are inevitably attracted by moist conditions. They can quickly devour young cabbage plants completely, or will nibble away at the inside leaves of mature plants, causing the rest to rot. To deter these pests, apply a sprinkling of long-lasting slug pellets to the surrounding soil, but to avoid damage to the hundreds of surface roots which a cabbage has, these pellets should not be raked into the soil.

PIGEONS start eating at the crack of dawn and are very partial to a feast of fresh cabbage leaves for breakfast. They will strip the leaves completely in a very short period of time, whether the cabbage plants are young or mature.

The only way to deter them is to spread netting over the whole cabbage patch. This should be suspended at least 1ft (30cm) above the cabbages. It does not matter what size mesh is used; pigeons will avoid going underneath any kind of netting.

SPLITTING is usually due to a heavy downpour of rain after a period of dry weather. The sudden uptake of liquid will be more than the plant can cope with, and its heart will split. To prevent this, try to keep the soil surrounding your giant cabbages moist at all times.

split cabbage heart

cabbage and bean medley

3oz (75g) butter or margarine
3lb (1.5kg) onion, peeled and
cut into rings
½ pint (300 ml) water
salt and pepper to taste
8oz (225g) broad beans removed
from the pods
2lb (900g) cabbage heart, shredded
2 apples, sliced
½ teaspoon mustard seeds

1. Melt the butter or margarine in a large saucepan and toss the onion rings in this (do not allow them to brown).
2. Add the water and bring to the boil. Season lightly, add the beans and simmer steadily for 5 minutes.
3. Add the shredded cabbage, apple slices and mustard seeds and cook for a further 5 minutes.
4. Drain and serve.

creamed cabbage

3lb (1.5kg) cabbage heart
2oz (50g) butter
2oz (50g) plain flour
1 pint (600ml) creamy milk
salt and pepper

1. Shred the cabbage and put it into boiling water. Boil for 10 minutes and drain very well, pressing out the moisture.
2. Melt the butter in a saucepan and work in the flour. Cook for 2 minutes, then gradually add the milk and seasoning.
3. Bring to the boil and simmer, stirring, for 5 minutes, then stir in the drained cabbage. Cook gently for about 10 minutes, then serve.

stuffed cabbage leaves

4 large cabbage leaves
2 tablespoons olive oil
1 large onion, peeled and finely chopped
8oz (225g) cooked chicken, minced
2 teaspoons chopped parsley
2 tablespoons sage and onion stuffing
½ level teaspooon tomato purée
½oz (12g) butter
7-8oz (200-225g) tinned tomatoes, chopped
salt, pepper, cumin

1. Trim the cabbage leaves into squares or rectangles; blanch them in boiling water for 3 minutes, drain thoroughly and leave to cool.
2. Heat the oil in a heavy-based pan; add the onions and cook over a low heat until transparent.
3. Stir in the meat, parsley, stuffing, tomato puree, 3 tablespoons boiling water, butter and chopped tomatoes.
4. Season with salt, pepper and a little cumin to taste, then simmer the mixture for 5-6 minutes.
5. Spread out the cabbage leaves, divide the filling equally between each and roll the leaves into tight parcels.
6. Place the stuffed leaves in a lightly buttered baking dish (joins down), cover the dish with foil and bake for 25 minutes in a preheated oven at 350°F, 180°C, Gas mark 4.
7. Serve with a thick tomato sauce.

glasshouse or propagator. If not, then early spring is a foolproof time.

Transplanting

Once the plants have reached 4–5in (10–12cm) in height, transplant the five strongest-looking specimens into their permanent growing positions in the centre of the wire netting, and set the remainder out 1ft (30cm) apart in the kitchen garden, to be used as 'greens' as soon as their leaves are big enough to make a meal.

Some form of wind protection should be provided for the five plants; a few pieces of glass 1ft (30cm) square pressed into the soil below the netting will do the trick.

Growth for autumn-sown plants will be slow over the winter months but at the first sign of spring the cabbages, already well established, will race away at an unbelievable rate.

Feeding

Cabbages should not be given any additional feed for at least a month after being transplanted. This allows the roots to develop fully, by travelling in all directions in search of the nutrients which are in the soil. In the fifth week, the transplanted cabbage plants should be starting to look healthy and strong, and this is the time for their first booster feed.

Most foliage plants thrive on high nitrogen feed and cabbages are no exception. A liquid feed is best, using a formula of 20N 10P 10K once every two weeks, as this will be instantly

available to the rooting system. This formula can be used right up until harvesting, unless the cabbage is showing a reluctance to heart up, when a single feed of 10N 10P 20K should be applied, before reverting to the normal high nitrogen feed.

Harvesting

Great care must be taken when harvesting a giant cabbage. It is very easy to break a leaf from a plant, and you must bear in mind that the outside leaves will be the biggest and heaviest. Each leaf may weigh 3 or 4lb (1.3 or 1.8kg), and this of course may make the difference between gaining first or second place in a competition.

It is difficult to harvest a giant cabbage by yourself if it measures in the region of 6ft (1.8m) across, so when the time comes I always invite a few of my friends around to give me a hand. Once the roots of the cabbage have been dug out of the ground from under the wire mesh, using a garden fork, the plant should be raised by everyone cupping their hands under the outside leaves and lifting it on to a 6ft (1.8m) square sheet of canvas or strong cloth.

The root, which to avoid dehydration should only be cut from the plant immediately before it is weighed, should be wrapped in damp cloths, with as much soil retained as possible, and placed in a waterproof polythene bag and tied securely. This will keep your prize specimen looking fresh for days. It can then be safely moved to its destination by four people lifting the corners of the canvas.

The rules for qualification to the record books are that a cabbage stalk must be trimmed as near to the main body of the plant as possible. It must also be free of any foreign bodies and be in a sound condition.

Bernard's giant cabbage patch

chapter six

onions

Onions have been cultivated from ancient times and are believed to have come originally from Asia. They were well known in Egypt in the time of the Pharaohs, and are now grown throughout the world in vast quantities.

This is a vegetable that gardeners all over the world try to grow to an enormous size. Giant onion championships take place everywhere, some with huge cash prizes and others with only much sought-after certificates. There are tales of exhibitors guarding their giant onions every night for months before a show, armed with all kinds of weapons from shotguns to spears. The rivalry is at times so intense that it is difficult for a non-competitor to begin to comprehend.

Onions are, however, one of the most expensive kinds of vegetable to grow to a giant size. This is because they must be kept at a temperature of 65° F (18° C) from mid winter until the early spring. Onions take from thirty-six to forty weeks from seed-sowing to harvesting.

I readily admit to a weakness for onions; I enjoy eating them in any shape or form, and would happily eat them 365 days a year. I like them boiled, baked, fried, grilled and roasted, as well as raw with sandwiches or salads. They make an excellent flavouring for soups, casseroles and stews and are an essential ingredient of many sauces (some recipes are given on page 60).

An onion weighing 12lb 4oz (5.58kg) was grown in 1994 by Mr Mel Ednie of Anstruther, Fife, Scotland.

Planning ahead

The ideal situation for onion plants is an open, sunny position free from the shade of trees or buildings in the late afternoon. Some type of windbreak will also be needed to prevent the onion's tender leaves from being damaged. Each plant will need an area of approximately 2ft (60cm) square, with a walkway of 1ft (30cm) between each row.

Soil preparation

A rich light soil with lots of humus and a pH of around 6.8 will provide ideal conditions in which to grow giant onions. The ground should be deeply dug in the autumn, and if you are using a rotation method, you should use the area which was limed the previous year for brassicas. Onions, however, are one of the few vegetables which can be grown successfully, year after year, in the same soil, provided it remains disease-free. If a raised bed system is used, the structure of the growing mixture can easily be improved by adding extra humus every year.

Seeds

It is absolutely essential to obtain the correct variety of seeds if you intend to grow giant onions, and there are many readily available varieties sold throughout the world that have the essential genetic potential to grow giant

ONION HAZARDS

THRIPS are very destructive to the foliage of onions. The adults are small and slender, varying in colour from yellow to brown. They feed on the sap in the foliage, and this results in light or mottled areas appearing between the veins. They also lay their eggs in the plant's foliage, and as they breed

*Thrip damage seen
inside an onion*

continuously throughout the year, they will devastate your entire onion bed if left unchecked.

To produce massive bulbs onions must have strong, healthy, undamaged foliage, so make sure that the insecticide used in your spraying programme deals with thrips.

ONION MILDEW or **DOWNY MILDEW** is a disease which attacks onions which are grown too close together and do not have adequate air circulation. It may also occur during prolonged spells of damp and misty weather.

The symptoms are leaves dying from the tips and eventually withering, rendering the plant useless. The disease can be cured if the plant is sprayed with a suitable fungicide at the first signs of infection, but prevention is certainly better than cure, and your spraying programme should help to keep this menace at bay.

ONION FLY is without doubt the most serious pest, and it is particularly destructive in the spring and early summer when the plants are young. The fly will lay its tiny white eggs on the neck of the onion bulb and the resulting maggots will attack the base of the bulb before travelling along the row of onions, destroying them one by one.

The first signs of an infestation are yellowing of the leaves, followed by the complete collapse of the plant. Infected plants should

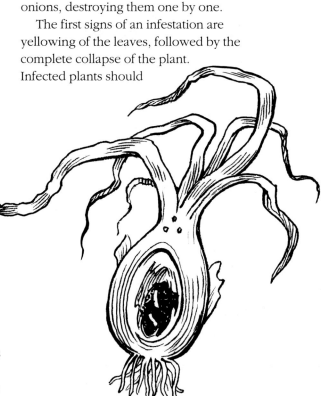

*Damage by onion fly larvae seen from
inside the bulb*

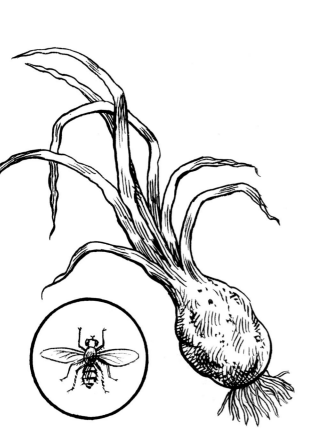

An onion infected by onion fly becomes misshapen and eventually collapses.

be dug up immediately, put in a plastic bag and relegated to the dustbin – never the compost heap. Your regular spraying programme will help to deter this fly, but an additional two-weekly dusting of the surrounding soil with an insecticide powder between sprayings should guarantee immunity.

GENERAL ADVICE If, for any reason at all, an onion plant stops growing, or the bulb starts to rot or go soft, the wisest course of action is always to dig the onion up and put both the plant and the surrounding soil into a dustbin.

onions. However, even if they are grown from the same packet of seeds, onions will inevitably vary considerably in size by the time they are harvested, and consequently I always grow at least four times as many onion plants as the number of prize specimens I eventually hope to have.

Unlike most other vegetables, onion seeds do not have a long storage life, and the germination rate will fall dramatically after the second year.

Sowing the seeds

Timing is a crucial element when growing giant onions, and where you live will determine how early the plants can be transplanted into the open garden soil.

To prevent the seedlings becoming too big and therefore easily damaged, you should allow approximately 100 days between sowing the seeds and transplanting the seedlings. I always sow my first batch of seeds in mid-winter, and a second back-up batch in late winter in case of failure.

The seeds should be covered with a seed dressing powder before being sown ¼in (6mm) deep in a tray of a peat-based compost, and placed in an electric propagator with a bottom heat of 65°F (18°C). They should germinate in about twenty-one days, with the first leaf protruding through the compost in a doubled up manner.

When they have reached this 'crooked stage', I lift the seedlings out of their tray and pot each one on into a 3in (7cm) plant pot of a similar compost. These are then put on the glasshouse bench in full light and with an air temperature of 60°F (15°C). When the roots start to grow through the bottom of the pots I move them on into individual 6in (15cm) pots, again in similar compost, being careful not to disturb the rootball as I do so.

No additional feed should be applied to the young plants while they are growing in the pots, as the fertilizer already present in the compost should be enough to last them until transplanting time.

sage and onion tart

8oz (225g) shortcrust pastry
1 giant-sized onion (weighing
about 4lb/1.8kg), peeled and chopped
1oz (25g) butter
¼ pint (150ml) creamy milk
1 egg
1 tablespoon chopped fresh sage
1 tablespoon chopped fresh parsley
4oz (115g) rindless bacon, chopped
salt and pepper

*1. Line an 8in (20cm) pie plate
with the rolled-out pastry.*
*2. Toss the chopped onion in the hot butter
until soft, then place it in the bottom of the
pastry case.*
*3. Mix the milk, eggs, herbs, chopped bacon
and seasoning together, and pour into the
pastry case.*
*4. Bake at 400°F, 200°C, Gas mark 6 for
30-35 minutes.*

cucumber and onion ragout

1 large cucumber (4lb/1.8kg), sliced
*1 giant onion (about 3lb/1.5kg), peeled
and finely chopped*
2oz (50g) butter
3 tablespoons flour
salt and pepper
¼ pint (150ml) wine or chicken stock

*1. Heat the butter in a large frying pan
and fry cucumber slices and onions gently
for 10 minutes.*
*2. Shake the flour, seasoned with a little salt
and pepper, over the vegetables; stir well
to blend.*
*3. Pour the wine or chicken stock into the
pan, then cover and simmer for 8 minutes.*
*4. Remove the lid and continue cooking for
3-4 minutes so any excess liquid evaporates.*
*5. Top with chopped parsley and chopped
chives and garnish with triangles of toast.*

Transplanting

A 6in (15cm) hole should be dug in the centre of each plant's allocated 2ft (60cm) square before the plant is carefully removed from the pot. Once the onion plant has been transplanted into position and firmed down, it should be covered by a further 1in (2.5cm) layer of soil.

You should then push 4ft (1.2m) canes into the ground at each corner of the plant's growing area, and wind string round the four canes from bottom to top at approximately 6in (15cm) intervals. This will support the onion leaves as they grow, and help to prevent them from bending in the wind.

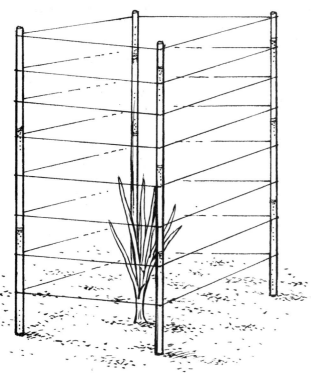

For each onion plant, a 'cage' is constructed with 4ft (1.2m) canes inserted in the ground at each corner, and horizontal strings 6in (15cm) apart wound round them to support the growing leaves.

Another successful giant onion harvest

onions, making foliar feeding difficult; the preferable solution is to mix a wetting agent (carefully following the manufacturer's instructions) with a ¼ strength liquid feed, and administer it in a very fine spray.

Spraying

A regular two-weekly spraying programme should commence a week after the onion plants have been transplanted, and this should continue right up until harvesting time. A systemic insecticide and fungicide should be used to cover all the hazards listed below, and a regular sprinkling of slug pellets around each plant is also advisable.

Harvesting

An onion plant will let you know when it has finished growing. The neck goes soft and lifeless just above the bulb, and the foliage would collapse without the string and cane supports.

To avoid dehydration and possible weight loss, I always leave my giant onions in the ground for as long as possible before the date of the show. Only if a few days of damp misty weather were forecast, and the onion had stopped growing, would I harvest it and hang it up by the foliage in a well ventilated shed. The foliage should not be cut off until just before the onion is weighed.

The qualification for entry into the record books requires that an onion's foliage must be trimmed above the top of the bulb at or below the first leaf joint. The roots must be removed, and the onion should be in a sound condition and free from any dirt or foreign bodies.

Feeding

Feeding should begin two weeks after the plants have been transplanted to their permanent growing positions. They will need a high nitrogen liquid formula of 20N 10P 10K, and this should be repeated every two weeks until the middle of summer, when the formula should be changed to a high potash one of 10N 10P 20K. The extra potash will help the onions to bulk up and put on the extra weight that is required.

Water tends to run off the shiny leaves of

chapter seven

radishes

Radishes are hardy and quick-growing annuals, cultivated from very early times for their fleshy root which was eaten raw.

There are now dozens of summer varieties of radish, ranging from very small round deep red ones, to the much larger Japanese white mooly varieties. There is also a selection of winter-hardy radishes, including black, pink and white ones.

To many people the very idea of a giant radish is ridiculous, but to a giant vegetable grower it is just another challenge. I can remember when I first broke the world record with a long white mooly radish weighing 28lb 1oz (12.98kg). It took me nearly an hour to dig it out of its bed by hand. I was afraid of snapping off some of its smaller roots, and my heart was pounding from start to finish. When the operation was successfully completed the radish measured over 3ft (90cm) long, and the top was as thick as my thigh.

This particular prize specimen was never eaten, because after it had been authenticated as a world record and completed its triumphant tour of duty, I used it in my seed-breeding programme to improve the original variety.

Although most radishes are eaten with salads, they are also superb when cooked. My favourite recipe, which I often use for the large white radishes, is to serve them mashed with a cooked meal. I remove the outside skin, dice the flesh into ½ in (12mm) cubes, boil them for ten minutes, drain off the water, add a little butter and pepper, and mash them.

Planning ahead

Giant white radish will grow well in deep, well cultivated sandy soil, but for the best results I recommend that you grow them in raised beds at least 2ft 6in (75cm) high. Two old doors, laid on their sides and with 2ft (60cm) pieces of wood nailed across the ends, would make an ideal home for four giant radish plants.

Radishes belong to the brassica family and although they will usually grow in any type of soil, better results are achieved with a pH level of 7–7.5. Radishes should only be grown for two consecutive years in the raised bed, before being followed by carrots, parsnips or onions.

Seeds

The seeds for giant radishes can be purchased from any garden centre or seed catalogue. When radish seeds are harvested in large quantities the pods are dried out and then milled to separate the seed from the chaff. The size of the seeds in a packet will probably vary considerably, reflecting the size

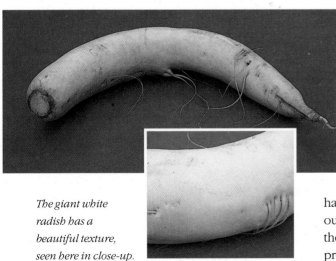

The giant white radish has a beautiful texture, seen here in close-up.

RADISH HAZARDS

APHIDS are a common enemy of radishes. Select a chemical that is suitable for cucumbers and that will deal with green, white and black fly, and with mealy bugs.

ROOT FLY can attack at any time of the year. Your spraying programme should deter this pest, but an additional sprinkling of a soil insecticide powder on the surrounding soil should ensure complete safety for your plant.

GREY MOULD (Botrytis) can cause serious damage and will invade any damaged part of the plant. An outside radish leaf will often turn yellow and die when the plant has finished with it, and if this is not removed, grey mould will attack it and spread quickly to the rest of the plant. A daily plant inspection is the most effective method I have found to keep this disease at bay.

CATERPILLARS can strip the leaves to a skeleton overnight. Butterflies will often lay their clusters of yellow eggs on or underneath the leaves of a radish, and these must be removed as soon as possible by rubbing them off with your fingers.

SLUGS AND SNAILS hide in the soil and will attack the radish leaves, as well as gnawing chunks from the side of the roots, which may then start to rot. Sprinkle a few long-lasting slug pellets regularly near the roots of each plant.

SPLITTING will result if the soil or growing mixture is allowed to dry out and is then watered heavily. The plant will not be able to cope with the sudden uptake of liquid, and its root may split. It may then be attacked by flies or fungi.

to which the seeding stock plants grew. It is therefore very important that only the largest seeds from a packet are used for your giant radishes; the remainder can be grown for the kitchen. If radish seeds are stored in an airtight container at room temperature, they will keep for at least five years.

Sowing the seeds

Timing is very important if you require a specimen for a particular date. You should allow ninety to one hundred days between seed sowing and harvesting; after this a radish will go quickly to seed and will be useless for showing.

A cluster of four seeds should be sown ½in (12mm) deep, directly into the ground or into the growing mixture of the raised bed, at each plant's proposed growing station. The whole area should then be watered and sprinkled with a soil insecticide powder.

The seeds should germinate in three or four days, and as soon as it is clear which is the strongest plant of each cluster, the other three can be discarded.

There are several different shapes of radish, the most common being, from left to right, French Breakfast, Mooly and Round Salad.

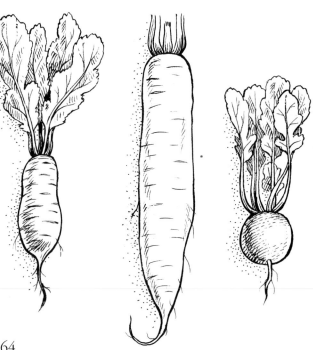

Feeding

Unlike many other brassicas radishes are not gross feeders and do not respond to a high nitrogen feed. I recommend a balanced feed of liquid fertilizer, with a formula of 20N 20P 20K, once a week from ten days after the final thinning right up until harvesting. A foliar feed of ⅛ strength can also be applied every few days, but you should never carry out this operation in full sunlight.

Spraying

The leaves of a radish plant are very tender indeed, and great care should be exercised when selecting chemicals for spraying. I always choose one that is suitable for cucumbers, as radish leaves are very similar to those of the cucumber.

To keep at bay the many pests and diseases which attack this vegetable, you will need to carry out a fungicide and insecticide spraying programme every two weeks, from germination to harvesting.

Harvesting

Leave the harvesting until as late as possible if you are trying for that elusive heaviest record, or are taking your specimen to an exhibition or show. Carefully remove the surrounding soil or growing mixture, making sure that you do not break off any small side roots. Ask someone to support the foliage and prevent the radish falling over as you dig deeper towards the tip of its root. When it is clear of the ground, wash it thoroughly with a medium strength jet of water from the garden hose.

If you are travelling a long distance to a show, or it is in any way

Harvesting a giant white mooly radish grown in a raised bed. You should always leave the foliage on until just before the root is weighed.

inconvenient to leave the harvesting until the last minute, you can prevent dehydration by wrapping the root in wet towels after it has been cleaned. The foliage should be trimmed off the top of the radish just before the root is weighed.

The rules for entry in the record books are that a radish must be in a sound condition and free from sticks, stones or dirt, and that the foliage must be trimmed as near as possible to the shoulders of the radish root.

A radish weighing 37lb 15oz (17.2kg) was grown in 1992 by the Letterini family in Tanonda, South Australia.

cucumbers

Cucumbers are believed to be natives of Africa and the warmer parts of Asia. Grown for thousands of years, they are now produced worldwide in huge quantities as a salad vegetable.

There are many different types of cucumber. All are very low in calories and often used in weight-reducing diets, but their nutritional value is almost nil. The standard ridge varieties are the ones that are usually grown outdoors; they will grow along the top of the soil and do not require supports. The Japanese varieties are, however, the ones suited to glasshouse and polythene tunnel cultivation. The plants need to be trained to grow up canes and along supporting wires approximately 6ft (1.8m) above ground-level. I have found this the most successful method when growing giant cucumbers.

Planning ahead

Giant cucumbers will need a little more heat and humidity than most other glasshouse crops. Cucumber roots hate being cold or waterlogged, and to avoid this I grow my plants in raised beds. These can be made from strong wooden boxes with the top and bottom removed, and should be about 2ft (60cm) square. They should be placed on top of cultivated soil, with an overhead supporting wire directly above each one. Before a box is filled with growing mixture, a strong cane must be secured, running from the soil below its centre to the overhead wire support. Allow twenty to twenty-three weeks from seed sowing to harvesting.

If you are growing your cucumber plants in the ground and not in a raised bed, each plant will require a space about 2ft (60cm) x 10ft (3m). Since cucumber plants have a very tender root system, a walkway of wooden planks between the rows will be essential to prevent soil compaction and root damage.

Soil preparation

Cucumbers thrive in deep, rich, open soil with a pH of 6.7, and the soil for plants grown in the

Female flowers (left) have a small cucumber behind them; male flowers (below) should be removed as soon as they appear.

The most successful way of growing the Japanese varieties of giant cucumber is to train them up canes and along a system of supporting wires.

other for the longest. The record books also list these two categories.

'Zeppelin' is the best known variety of heavy cucumber, and 'Telegraph' the longest. Both varieties should be easily available, but if you can obtain seed from a specialist grower of giant vegetables, so much the better.

Pollination

Cucumbers are parthenocarpic, which means that vegetative growth will develop independently of fertilization. If a female flower is pollinated, the resulting cucumber will taste bitter, so commercial growers generally use F1 hybrid all-female varieties which remove the risk of pollination.

However, most giant cucumber varieties are open-pollinated and will produce both male and female flowers in abundance, and unless you require a cucumber for seed, the male flowers should be removed as soon as they appear. Male flowers will have just a thin stem, while female flowers will have small cucumbers behind them.

If you do require a plant for its seeds, I advise hand pollination. First cut the male flower from the plant and carefully remove its petals. Then press the stamen full of pollen gently into the centre of the female flower, and pollination should be complete. Leave the resulting cucumber until it has ripened to a yellow colour, at which point the seeds should be ready to harvest.

ground should have a high humus content. A few bags of sphagnum peat make a good substitute if you do not have access to sterilized compost, though this may alter the pH level, and a dusting of lime may be required to bring it up to the recommended 6.7 reading. The soil, whether for plants grown directly in the ground or in raised beds above, should be well cultivated. For raised beds I use a growing mixture of 50/50 peat and soil.

Seeds

There are two different classes for cucumbers at most 'giant' shows: one for the heaviest and the

Sowing the seeds

A cucumber seed should be sown on its edge, ¼ in (6mm) deep, in a 3in (7cm) plant pot containing a peat-based compost. It should then

A cucmber weighing 20lb 1oz (9kg) was grown in 1991 by Mr Bernard Lavery in Llanharry, South Wales.

68

be thoroughly watered and placed in a propagator set at 70° F (21° C). If you do not have a propagator, cover the top of the plant pot with a small clear plastic bag, held in place with a rubber band, and place it in the airing cupboard. The seeds should start to germinate after three or four days, when the pots should be removed from the heat and placed in full daylight on the glasshouse bench with an air temperature of 60° F (15° C).

I always sow a few extra seeds two weeks after the main batch, to provide a back-up in case of unforeseen disasters.

Transplanting

Once the plants have grown four leaves, they can be transplanted into their permanent growing positions alongside the supporting canes, either in a raised bed or in the ground. They will take a few days to settle down in their new homes, but after that they will grow very quickly.

Growing on

At this stage any developing flowers and laterals (side shoots) must be removed as they appear, and the main growing stem secured to the vertical cane every 9in (23cm) as it grows.

When the growing tip reaches the horizontal supporting wire, the plant should be trained along it by tying the stem to the wire at 4in (10cm) intervals. Female flowers should now be left to develop, and only the male ones removed.

The growing tip of the plant should be pinched out when it reaches the end of its wire, and all the cucumbers removed apart from the strongest-looking one. As this cucumber grows, it will become very heavy and should be supported with a piece of soft netting from the overhead wire, allowing the netting to take about half the cucumber's weight. This will prevent the plant from becoming stressed, while letting it know that it has not quite finished its job. As the cucumber continues to grow, slacken the netting slightly, so that it continues to support only half the weight.

CUCUMBER HAZARDS

POWDERY MILDEW flourishes in these humid conditions. The top of the cucumber leaves become covered with a white powdery mould which will spread through the whole glasshouse if left unchecked. Fortunately, it can be cured if a fungicide spray is applied as soon as the disease is discovered.

GREY MOULD (Botrytis) is another disease of humid conditions. It will attack any damaged parts of of the plant, depositing a grey mould which quickly spreads. There is no cure for grey mould if it takes a real hold, but your regular spraying programme should keep the disease at bay.

MOSAIC VIRUS is a common but extremely serious disease. The virus is spread by greenfly, and as there is no cure for infected plants, they should be removed and relegated to the dustbin as soon as the problem is identified. Your regular spraying programme should again provide some protection.

RED SPIDER MITE is very difficult to eradicate. The mites require a strong chemical to kill them, and there are few of these that a tender cucumber plant can tolerate. However, the deadly pests hate damp conditions, and will first gain a foothold on the dry leaves at the top of the plants nearest the glass roof. The best deterrent is to make sure that these leaves have a regular and thorough daily soaking.

OVERWATERING can cause a cucumber's roots to rot, so you should always ensure that the soil does not become waterlogged.

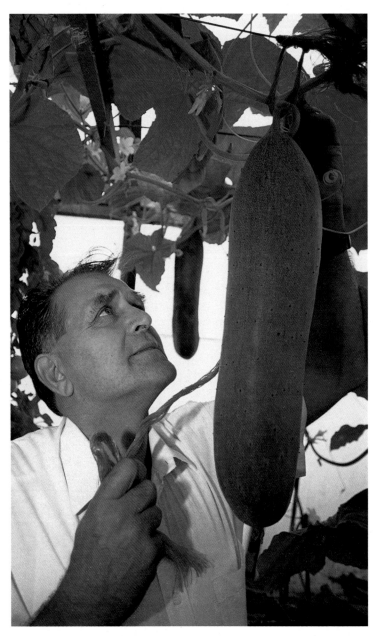

Adjusting the string supports to take the increasing weight of the cucumber.

thrive on humidity, a tepid fresh-water mist spray should be applied once or twice a day.

If you are growing your plants directly in the glasshouse soil, make sure that the soil does not become waterlogged. Plants in raised beds will not encounter this problem.

Spraying

The high humidity and damp conditions that a cucumber plant enjoys are, unfortunately, the same conditions that encourage many diseases. It is important therefore to make regular applications of an insecticide and fungicide spray. The leaves of cucumber plants are very tender, and it is essential to use only the chemicals that manufacturers recommend, and to follow their directions to the letter.

Harvesting

Freshly harvested young cucumbers are delicious in sandwiches or with a salad. However, if you are aiming for the heaviest or the longest, I am afraid that by the time you harvest your prize specimen, it will probably be too tough to eat.

Cucumbers should be kept growing for as long as possible, and to prevent dehydration should be harvested only hours before being weighed or measured. If for any reason you need to harvest yours early, you can cut the stem 2ft (60cm) on each side of the cucumber, and place the two ends in a bucket of water.

To qualify for the record books, a cucumber can be of any colour, must be in a sound condition, and have not more than 1in (2.5cm) of stalk still attached to it.

Feeding

The roots of a cucumber plant will need a regular supply of high nitrogen liquid feed every two weeks throughout the growing season; I recommend a formula of 20N 10P 10K. A foliar feed of ⅛ strength of this mixture can be administered twice a week, and since the plants

70

cucumber creams

1 packet of lime jelly
1 teaspoon salt
2 tablespoons white wine vinegar
1 teaspoon grated onion
pepper
¼ pint (150ml) soured cream
¼ pint (150ml) mayonnaise
1 large cucumber (3lb/1.5kg), peeled, grated and drained
lettuce leaves to serve

1. Dissolve the jelly and salt in ¼ pint (150ml) boiling water.
2. Stir in the vinegar, onion and pepper, then chill until almost set.
3. Mix in the mayonnaise and soured cream, then fold in the cucumber. Turn into individual moulds; chill until set.
4. To serve, line individual serving plates with lettuce leaves; turn out the creams.

cucumber au gratin

1 large (3lb/1.5kg) cucumber, peeled
2oz (50g) butter
salt and freshly ground black pepper
6oz (150g) grated Gruyère cheese

1. Cut the cucumber into 3in (7.5cm) pieces, slice each in half lengthways and remove the seeds.
2. Simmer in boiling water for about 10 minutes. Drain, dry and place a layer in the base of a buttered fireproof dish.
3. Season with salt and pepper, then sprinkle with a third of the cheese.
4. Repeat the layers, finishing with cheese. Dot with butter.
5. Bake in the centre of a preheated oven at 400°F, 200°C, Gas mark 6, for about 30 minutes or until brown on top.

cucumber soup

1 large cucumber
2oz (50g) butter
2 tablespoons flour
1 pint (600ml) chicken stock or water
salt and pepper
½ pint (300ml) milk
1 egg
4 tablespoons double cream

1. Peel the cucumber and cut it in half, lengthways. Remove seeds and cut into small pieces.
2. Melt the butter in a heavy based saucepan and stir in the flour. Gradually add the stock or water and bring to the boil.
3. Add the cucumber and salt and pepper to taste; simmer until the cucumber is tender.
4. Sieve the soup, pressing the cucumber, to make a thin purée. Return to the pan.
5. In a small saucepan, heat the milk and stir it into the soup. Bring to simmering point, then remove from the heat.
6. Beat the egg with the cream and stir into the soup. Serve, garnished with parsley.

iced cucumber soup

1 large (3lb/1.5kg) cucumber, peeled and grated
15 fl oz (425g) natural yoghurt
1½ tablespoons tarragon vinegar
2½ tablespoons chopped chives
salt and pepper
3 tablespoons finely chopped gherkins
3oz (75g) shelled prawns

1. Mix together the cucumber, yoghurt, vinegar, chives and seasoning. Liquidize if you want a smooth texture.
2. Chill well. Stir in the gherkins and prawns just before serving.

chapter nine

celery

Celery is usually grown for its blanched leaf stalks, which are used in salads. It is also eaten as a cooked vegetable, and often used as a flavouring or soup ingredient.

There are dozens of new self-blanching varieties of celery which can be purchased from seed companies throughout the world, but these cannot equal the old-fashioned varieties in terms of flavour and size.

Planning ahead

Growing celery the traditional way is one of the most time-consuming and labour-intensive tasks a gardener can undertake, and although other methods are used to grow giant celery, considerable effort will still be required. The roots of a celery plant will go down about 18in (45cm) and can measure up to 3ft (90cm) across. They consist of thousands of very small tap roots which will tangle up with each other in their frantic search for nourishment.

Soil preparation

You will probably grow your celery in garden soil, and I recommend that you dig a trench 1ft (30cm) deep by 1ft (30cm) wide, and fill it

Unless you grow celery plants in a raised bed (see left), the best method is to dig a trench 1ft (30cm) deep and wide and fill it with a rich mixture of soil and well rotted organic matter.

with an equal mixture of one-third well rotted farmyard manure, one-third composted material or peat, and one-third soil. This should be done in the autumn and left to overwinter. An ideal pH reading for growing celery is 6.5, and you may have to adjust your soil in the spring by sprinkling lime to raise the level, or digging in a little extra composted material or peat to lower it. Plants need to be spaced 3ft (90cm) apart, and to calculate how long the trench should be, you must first decide how many plants you intend to grow.

I prefer to use the raised bed system when growing my giant celery and I find that half a 45-gallon (200 litre) drum, the end removed, provides the ideal home for a giant celery plant. A similar growing mixture to the one already described for trenching can be used to fill them once they are positioned on top of the soil. The advantage is that the roots in the raised bed system will have excellent drainage and at least 2ft (60cm) of first-class growing mixture to forage through before even reaching the cultivated topsoil underneath, while the bottom of a trench may suffer as a result of poorly draining subsoil.

Seeds

Each celery plant will produce over 200,000 seeds in the second year of growth, and

Transplant celery seedlings into individual 3in (7cm) pots once they have made two strong primary leaves.

A strong root system is essential when growing celery for size.

if these are kept in an airtight container at room temperature, they should keep in a sound condition for at least seven years.

Seed of many old types of giant celery seed can be purchased throughout the world, but the commonest and probably the best is 'Ideal'. This variety will grow to a height of 4ft (1.2m) and has a mainly light green stem with just a trace of pink.

For table use, the timescale from seed sowing to harvesting is approximately five months, by which time the young stems should be crisp and extremely tasty (see recipes on page 77). But if you are growing them for competition or exhibition, the plants will have to be kept growing for as long as possible. Those grown from Thiram-treated seed sown in late winter can usually be held in the ground until early autumn, though they will unfortunately be inedible by then.

A celery weighing 46lb 1oz (20.7kg) was grown in 1990 by Bernard Lavery in Llanharry, South Wales.

Sowing the seeds

Late winter is the best time to make your first sowing of celery seeds. They should be sprinkled on top of a peat-based compost and then watered in thoroughly before being placed in an electric propagator with a bottom heat of 75° F (24° C). If you do not have a propagator and night time temperatures are dropping below freezing, wait until early spring before sowing the seed.

The seeds should take eighteen to twenty days to germinate; immediately this occurs, the heat should be reduced to 65° F (18° C). If your propagator thermostat cannot be adjusted, put a layer of cardboard or polystyrene under the pots to absorb the heat.

As soon as the seedlings have made two strong primary leaves, they should be potted on into individual 3in (7cm) plant pots filled with the same kind of peat-based compost as for the sowing medium. They can then be placed on the glasshouse bench in full daylight. To avoid any check to the plants' growth, it is extremely important to keep the growing compost moist at all times.

CELERY HAZARDS

CENTRE HEART ROT is a terminal disease. It develops following damage caused by pests such as earwigs, slugs, snails, woodlice and worms feeding on and boring holes into the tender new celery leaves at the centre of the plant. Your spraying programme, together with a sprinkling of soil insecticide powder and slug pellets, should help deter the predators and so eliminate the disease.

SLUGS AND SNAILS will be attracted to the moist soil in great numbers. A regular sprinkling of mini slug pellets should be applied to the soil throughout the season.

CELERY FLY females will lay dozens of minute eggs on or within the plant's leaves, usually in mid-spring, mid- and then late summer. These will result in small maggots which burrow into the leaf tissues, causing blisters and loss of vigour, and greatly affecting the growth of your plants. The infected leaves should be removed immediately they are discovered, but you should not be bothered by these insects at all provided you adhere to a two-weekly spraying programme.

LEAF SPOT is carried by seeds, and as a precaution 'Thiram' treated seeds should always be used. It can be identified very early in a celery plant's life by brown spots forming on the outside leaves, so always inspect your seedlings before transplanting, and discard any suspect plants. In a wet season leaf spot can quickly destroy the whole plant, but spraying with the correct fungicide mixture as soon as it is discovered should eliminate the disease.

WIND DAMAGE Use a windbreak when growing celery in an exposed condition to avoid the risk of damage from strong winds.

Transplanting

When the plants are approximately 3in (7cm) high and the weather conditions are settled, they should be transplanted to their permanent growing positions. Six 4ft (1.2m) long canes should be pushed firmly into the ground to form a 3ft (90cm) diameter circle around each plant, and string should be tied horizontally around the canes at 6in (15cm) intervals. This will help to support the celery leaves as the plant grows, and will eliminate the need for blanching covers or heaping soil against the plants for support.

Feeding

Celery plants need a constant supply of water, and the soil surrounding their roots should never be allowed to dry out. Each plant will send out hundreds of little surface roots that will be waiting to take up the moisture from even the lightest of showers or early morning dew. If these roots are kept constantly watered, you are already halfway to growing a monster celery plant. From the second week after transplanting, the plants will need a high nitrogen feed, with a formula of 20N 15P 10K, once a week until harvesting.

Spraying

A spraying programme using a fungicide and insecticide mixture should be carried out once every two weeks throughout the growing season, to deter the pests and diseases described above.

Harvesting

Harvesting a giant celery plant single-handed can be an awesome task, so I advise you to

When transplanting a young celery plant into a raised bed or a trench in the ground, be especially careful to keep the rootball intact.

soil at several points around the root at an angle of 45 degrees, and cut sideways as far as you can. In this way the plant can be released from the ground with just enough of its root remaining to keep the celery fresh and healthy-looking until it is required. Place the roots in a bucket containing 4in (10cm) of water, and do not trim them off until the last possible moment before the celery plant is weighed.

To qualify for the record books, a celery plant must have had all its roots removed and must be in a generally sound condition. The plant must also be free from dirt, sticks and stones or any other foreign bodies.

invite one or two friends along to lend a hand. To avoid any of the plant's tender leaf stems drooping on to the ground when the supporting string and canes are removed (which may result in leaves detaching themselves from the plant), the leaves should be tied securely together before the supports themselves are removed.

Using thick cord or string, make your first tie 1ft (30cm) from the base of the plant, and subsequent ones all the way up the plant at 1ft (30cm) intervals. Once this has been done, and the supporting canes and string have been removed, the plant should be held vertical while the harvesting is carried out.

It is not necessary to dig out the whole of the plant's huge root system when harvesting the celery. Instead, insert a long sharp knife into the

To harvest a giant celery plant, cut the roots at an angle of 45 degrees just below the base of the stem, using a long, sharp knife inserted into the soil.

saddled celery

1 large head of celery, cleaned
4 bacon rashers, rinded
½ pint (300ml) cheese sauce
1oz (25g) hard cheese, grated
tomato slices to garnish

1. *Cook the whole head of celery in boiling water until tender. Drain well and divide into four bundles.*
2. *Wrap a bacon rasher around each bundle and arrange them in a baking dish. Pour over the cheese sauce and sprinkle the grated cheese on top.*
3. *Bake in a pre-heated moderately hot oven (375°F, 190°C, Gas mark 5) for about 30-40 minutes.*
4. *Serve garnished with the tomato slices and parsley.*

the old celery sauce

This bland sauce was once very popular served with boiled turkey, pheasants and pigeons. It is also very good with braised loin of lamb.

1 large head of celery
1 onion, peeled and finely chopped
chicken stock
1 tablespoon butter
1 tablespoon flour

1. *Wash, string and chop the head of celery and cook it with the onion in enough stock to cover. Simmer with the lid on until the celery is tender.*
2. *Drain off and keep the liquor, then purée the onion and celery in the electric mixer or push them through a sieve.*
3. *Melt the butter, then stir in the flour. Gradually add about ½ pint (300ml) of the celery liquor, beating and stirring until the sauce is smooth and fairly thick.*
4. *Stir in the vegetable purée.*

cream of celery soup

1 heaped tablespoon butter
6 stalks of celery, washed and diced
several celery leaves, finely chopped
1 heaped tablespoon flour
1 pint (600ml) milk
bouquet garni
salt and pepper

1. *Melt the butter in a saucepan and gently sauté the diced celery and leaves until tender, but not too soft.*
2. *Add the flour and cook gently until it absorbs the butter.*
3. *Pour in the milk and bring to the boil, stirring continuously until soup thickens.*
4. *Add the bouquet garni and simmer gently for about 5 minutes.*
5. *Serve with croutons.*

curried celery salad

½ pint (300ml) thick mayonnaise
2 tablespoons lemon juice
1½ teaspoons curry powder
salt and pepper
1 head of celery weighing about 4lb (1.8kg), cleaned and sliced
9 spring onions, sliced
4oz (115g) sultanas

1. *Combine the mayonnaise, lemon juice and curry powder, then season with salt and pepper.*
2. *Fold in the celery, onions and sultanas.*
3. *Chill before serving.*

sweet melons

Sweet melons are grown in vast quantities in many parts of the world, doing best in warm climates. Growing giant melons is extremely easy, and they taste just as good as smaller ones.

Although melons are actually a fruit, they are classified as a vegetable for horticultural shows and judging purposes. They may be eaten on their own, with dried or smoked ham, or as an ingredient of fruit salads. They are very low in calories and are thus an ideal subject for diets. They are available in shops all year round, even though countries which experience winter frosts may have to import theirs from places thousands of miles away.

Cantaloupe and musk are the two most popular varieties of melon, and as the cantaloupe will grow much bigger, this is the type I grow.

Planning ahead

If you are growing giant melons in the open garden, the ideal site is a southerly facing plot with some wind protection. Melon plants require an endless supply of liquid, but must never be allowed to become waterlogged. Raised hillocks of soil and farmyard manure over cultivated soil will provide the necessary free-draining conditions, and these should be made in early spring, so that by the time your plants are ready to be set out, the manure will have started to decompose, creating extra warmth for the plants' roots.

Melons should not be subjected to temperatures lower than 40° F (4° C), so if you require an early or late crop, I advise you to grow them in a glasshouse, following the same method as for cucumbers. A small raised bed or wooden box with the top and bottom removed, placed on top of cultivated soil and filled with 50/50 mixture of peat and soil, would provide ideal conditions.

Soil preparation

The soil or growing mixtures for successful melon growing should be deeply dug and of a no-clay, free-draining structure. The small hillocks in the garden should consist of 6in (15cm) of manure, 6in (15cm) of soil, a further 6in (15cm) of manure and a final 1ft (30cm) of soil. However, I would never recommend the use of farmyard manure in a glasshouse, as the confined space and restricted air circulation may encourage pests and diseases to develop.

The ideal pH level for melons is 6.5, but I have grown some excellent specimens with a much lower lime level.

The female flower (far left) has a small melon behind the petals, as distinct from the male flower (left).

Secure your melon plant securely to its cane in stages as it grows, using soft twine.

Seeds

You must initially purchase seeds of a giant melon strain from a specialist supplier or grower; thereafter, you will be able to harvest seeds from one of your own mature cantaloupes and store them for use the following year.

Sowing the seeds

The average time from sowing the seed to harvesting the first melon is about twelve to fourteen weeks, but you should allow nearer twenty weeks for a single giant to be harvested. This timescale is important if you require a melon for a certain day of the year. The seeds should be sown on their edges, ½in (12mm)

deep in 3in (7cm) pots filled with a peat-based compost. Each pot should be thoroughly watered and placed in a propagator with a heat setting of 70° F (21° C). If you do not have this facility, cover each pot with a polythene bag secured with a rubber band, and place it in an airing cupboard or near the hot water tank. Germination should take place in six to eight days, and as soon as this occurs the pots should be brought out into full daylight – on a window sill or in the glasshouse – with a minimum temperature of 55° F (13° C). They should be kept continually moist, but not overwatered.

Transplanting

The seedlings can be transplanted into the garden once they have developed four leaves, and when weather conditions are favourable. It is better to keep the young plants on the glasshouse bench until they have grown eight or ten leaves than to transplant them into the garden too soon and finish up with plants damaged by cold winds or frost.

Growing on

The procedure for growing melons on differs according to whether you are growing the plants outdoors or indoors.

Outdoors Once it has cleared its growing mound, the main runner of a plant should be allowed to travel for a further 6ft (1.8m) along the top of the soil before its growing tip is cut off. Cut off the growing tips of the laterals (side shoots) when they have developed two leaves each. Sub-laterals will form from the base of these two leaves, and these should be allowed to grow for at least 6ft (1.8m) in either direction. These two sub-laterals will then produce an abundance of male and female flowers.

Indoors If you are growing your melon plants in a glasshouse, the same methods that are used for growing cucumbers should be followed. Each plant should be grown up a strong cane, with the laterals (side shoots) removed as soon as they develop, until the main growing stem reaches the overhead

80

SWEET MELON HAZARDS

RED SPIDER MITE thrive in the drier atmosphere of the glasshouse that melons, like tomatoes, require.

These tiny spiders are almost impossible to detect with the naked eye, but they can soon devastate a melon plant by drawing the sap from the undersides of the leaves, which will turn yellowish in colour and become very brittle. An infestation of red spider mite can sometimes be detected by a fine silky spider's web on a leaf.

Any damaged leaves should be carefully cut from the plant, placed in a polythene bag, and relegated to the dustbin. The plant should then be thoroughly sprayed with a suitable insecticide.

GREY MOULD and **POWDERY MILDEW** will sometimes cause havoc with melon plants, but your regular fungicide spraying programme should keep both of these diseases at bay.

ROOT ROT occurs if the plant's roots become too wet or waterlogged, or the surface of the soil or growing mixture is too cold. The disease is terminal, and infected plants should be discarded immediately. Leaving half the rootball above the soil's surface when transplanting is one way to help prevent the occurrence of root rot in your melon plants.

SPLITTING occurs when the melon experiences a sudden uptake of liquid after drought. If the soil surrounding a melon plant is allowed to dry out, it must be restored to a damp condition gradually. If, for example, a thunderstorm takes place after a dry period in the garden, the liquid uptake will be more than the plants can cope with, and the melons will inevitably split unless the soil has been well and regularly watered before the storm.

STRESS unavoidably occurs to the glasshouse melon plant when its suspended melon reaches about 5lb (2.25kg) in weight. The melon should be supported by a net as soon as it reaches the size of a medium-sized orange, and this will also prevent the stalk from breaking.

Use a net suspended from the overhead supports of a glasshouse to take the majority of the melon's weight.

supporting wires. At this point the laterals should be allowed to develop two leaves before being stopped, and the first sub-lateral should be allowed to develop and take over the role of being the main runner. When this sub-lateral has reached a length of 2ft (60cm), all the other growing tips, including the original main stem, should be removed. This will allow the new 'main runner' to develop into a very strong part of the plant and produce female flowers in abundance.

If you are attempting to grow an exceptionally big or record-breaking melon, only one or two fruit should be allowed to remain on each plant.

> A Cantaloupe melon weighing 62lb (28.1kg) was grown in 1991 by Mr G. Daughtridge in Rocky Mount, North Carolina, U.S.A.

Pollination

I recommend that you hand-pollinate the female flowers on both indoor and outdoor plants as they open up. The female flowers have small melons behind their petals; the male ones have only a stalk.

Place a very small paintbrush into the centre of a male flower to pick up a little pollen, and gently transfer the pollen from the loaded paintbrush to the centre of the female flower. Tie a polythene bag over the female flower of plants grown outdoors, to protect the newly pollinated stigma from strong winds or rain. Success can be judged if the developing melons grow to the size of golfballs.

Feeding

A weekly high nitrogen liquid feed with a formula of 20N 10P 10K will be required from the second week after transplanting, right up to the third week before harvesting, when a high potash feed of 10N 10P 20K should be applied to help ripen the melons.

An additional twice weekly ⅛ strength foliar feed will be beneficial, and this should be administered early in the morning. This will

melon and ginger preserve

1 large melon, weighing about 5lb (2.25kg)
granulated sugar
8oz (225g) crystallized ginger
the juice and finely grated rind of 4 lemons

1. Peel and seed the melon and cut the flesh into 1in (2.5cm) cubes.
2. Put into an ovenproof dish with lid, adding 1lb (450g) sugar to each 4lb (1.8kg) melon flesh. Leave for about 10 minutes in a cool oven (300°F, 150°C, Gas mark 2) until the melon is soft but not broken up.
3. Put the mixture into a preserving pan with the crystallized ginger, cut into cubes, and the juice of the lemons. Add another 3lb (1.5kg) sugar per 4lb (1.8kg) of melon.
4. Boil until the setting point is reached (about 25 minutes), adding the grated rind of the lemons just before this.
5. Bottle into warm, sterilized jars and allow to cool before putting on their lids.

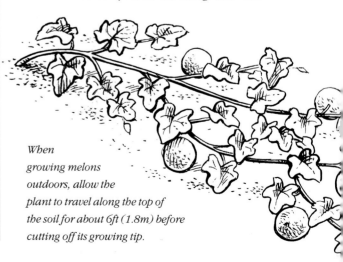

When growing melons outdoors, allow the plant to travel along the top of the soil for about 6ft (1.8m) before cutting off its growing tip.

Above: *Trim the growing tips of the laterals on a melon plant when they have developed two leaves each.*

Right: *To harvest a giant melon, use long-handled scissors or secateurs and cut through the stalk while supporting the melon's weight with the other hand.*

then allow the leaves to dry out during the daylight hours.

Spraying

A preventative spraying programme should be carried out every two weeks throughout the growing season. The leaves of melons are very tender, and great care must be taken to select fungicide and insecticide sprays that are suitable for use on melon plants. I advise using those sprays that are recommended for cucumbers.

Harvesting

As soon as a melon is ripe, it must be harvested; if it is left on the plant it will start to rot within days – which is why the timing is important

if you require a specimen for a special event.

The only way to extend the lifespan of a melon is to harvest it as soon as it starts to turn colour, and place it on a piece of cardboard in a refrigerator at a medium setting. It should keep in good condition for a month or six weeks in this way, though you may find that it loses a little in weight.

The regulations for entry into the record books are that a melon must be in a sound condition and that a maximum of 1in (2.5cm) of stalk be still attached to it.

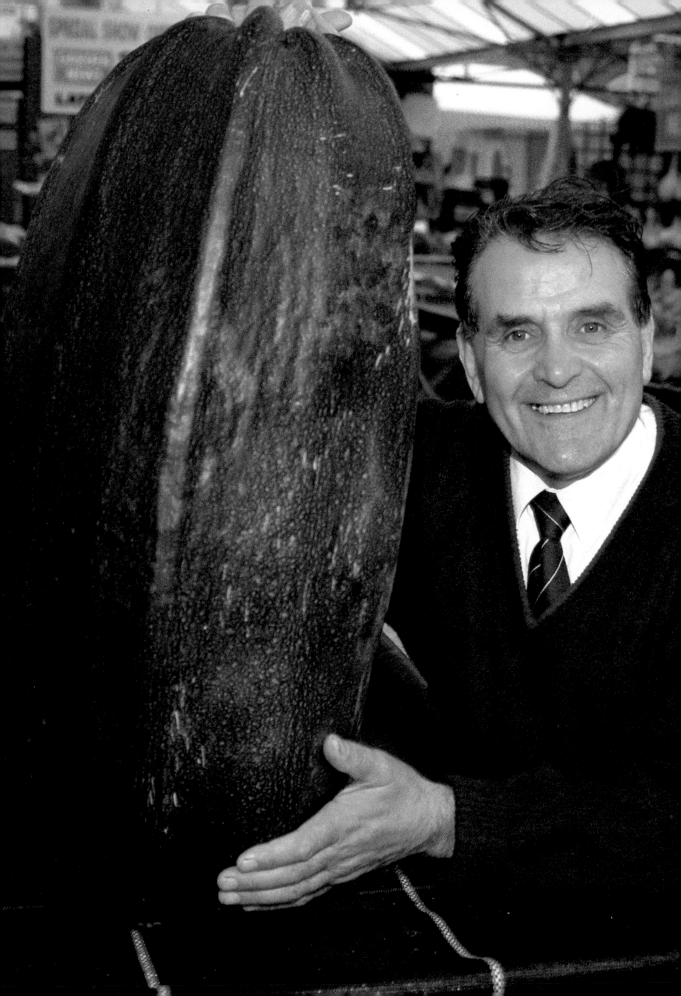

marrows

The marrow belongs to the gourd section of the cucurbit family.
It is one of the easiest of all the giants to grow, taking only
two and a half months from sowing the seed to harvesting.

I f you have never attempted to grow a giant marrow, I do urge you to have a go; you could end up with some real monsters that will amaze yourself as well as dumbfound your friends.

You may ask what you can do with a 3ft (90cm) long marrow weighing over 50lb (22kg)? The answer is, a number of things. You could share out 8lb (3.6kg) slices among your neighbours; you could eat the smaller ones from the same plant; and you can cook your marrow in a variety of ways. Marrows are good stuffed with minced meat or other chopped vegetables, and baked in the oven; they are good braised, boiled or flash fried; and they are a useful ingredient in making jams, chutney and wine (see the recipes on page 89).

This curious 'triple' marrow, weighing over 24lb (10.8kg), won first prize at a local horticultural show in 1932.

The male flower of a marrow.

Planning ahead

Marrows can be grown in a large glasshouse, in a polythene growing tunnel, or in the open garden. However, they do not like high temperatures in the daytime, and in most countries they grow better outdoors than in. Each plant will need a growing area of at least 6ft x 10ft (1.8m x 3m).

The roots of marrow plants are very tender, and a raised bed 1ft (30cm) high at the end of each allocated area, filled with a mixture of 75 per cent peat and 25 per cent soil, will provide the plant with ideal conditions in which to develop as strong and vigorous a root system as possible.

An alternative is to dig a 3ft (90cm) square hole, 1ft (30cm) deep, and fill it with some of your best compost. As a marrow plant will send out dozens of little surface roots, duck boards, or planks of wood to walk on, are essential to avoid damaging them.

If you do decide to grow your marrows under cover, you should whiten the overhead glass or polythene with a cool-glass mixture.

This will lower the summer temperature by about 10° F (6° C) and will help to prevent sun scorch to the leaves of the plant.

Raised beds are really essential when growing marrows under cover; they should be laid out and filled with the same mixture as for the outdoor beds. They can then be watered heavily without waterlogging, and the soil underneath will be kept moist, even on the hottest of days. For each fully developed marrow, you should allow ten to twelve weeks from seed sowing to harvesting.

Soil preparation

The underlying soil should be deep dug, and a large amount of humus or peat incorporated into the whole growing area. The pH of the growing mixture and soil should be as near as possible to 6.2.

Seeds

Two types of marrow are grown worldwide: 'bush' and 'trailing'. The trailing variety will usually grow much bigger than the bush type, so these are the ones I use to grow giants. It is essential that you shop around when purchasing seeds for growing

giant marrows. The best option is to obtain seeds from a specialist grower, who will only harvest the seeds from the heaviest specimens.

Sowing the seeds

The first sowing should be made in mid-spring, and the second one, as a back-up, a few weeks later. The seeds should be sown with the blunt end down and the curved end up, 1in (2.5cm) deep, into the centre of a 5in (12cm) pot of peat-based compost. These should be placed in a propagator with a heat setting of 70° F (21° C). The seeds should germinate in six to eight days, and as soon as this occurs, the pots can be moved to a position where they have the benefit of full daylight.

Transplanting

When the marrow plants have developed six leaves they should be transplanted to their permanent growing positions, and the outdoor ones sheltered with pieces of glass or plastic cloches. These windbreaks can be removed as soon as the plants start growing, or when weather conditions allow.

Uniformed Civil Defence workers proudly exhibit their marrows at a village vegetable show in 1941.

MARROW HAZARDS

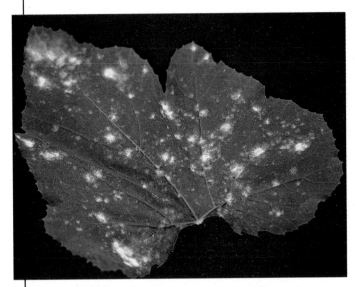

fungicide mixture. Severely infected plants should be relegated to the compost heap.

RED SPIDER MITE can devastate a marrow plant in a very short space of time if left unchecked. This pest will seldom attack marrows growing in the garden, but will thrive on plants growing in the arid conditions of glasshouses and growing tunnels.

The red spider mite extracts sap from the veins on the undersides of the plant's leaves, and an infestation can be identified by the leaves changing colour from green to yellow.

Infected leaves should be carefully removed into a polythene bag before being placed in the dustbin. An application of a suitable insecticide spray should then be made to the remainder of the plant, and repeated after five days.

POWDERY MILDEW is a marrow plant's worst enemy. It can develop in a very short space of time following damp misty weather, and is quite common towards the end of the year when night time temperatures are lower.

It can be identified by a white powdery covering on the top of the plant's leaves. If unchecked, the disease will very quickly spread to the whole plant, which will soon lose its vigour and eventually stop growing altogether.

The mildew can be eliminated by spraying with a suitable fungicide mixture as soon as the disease is discovered.

GREY MOULD (Botrytis) can attack the flower ends of marrows as well as any damaged parts of the plant. Loose leaves or any plant debris left on the soil will encourage the disease to develop, and it will soon spread to adjacent plants.

The disease can be identified by a grey mould covering infected parts of vegetables and plants, and can be eliminated, if treated early, by a thorough spraying of a suitable

MICE will come in from the garden at the end of summer, and make their winter homes in outbuildings or in the soil of glasshouses and growing tunnels. A mouse will often gnaw away at the outside skin of a marrow, and sometimes even bore a hole right inside it, to reach the hundreds of fresh seeds there.

I always place a small shallow tin of poisoned mouse bait by the side of each marrow in late summer, and make a daily check to see if any has been taken. It is important to replenish the bait before the mice move on to eat the marrow.

Growing on

As the main growing stem travels along the top of the ground, it should be covered over with a few inches (7–10cm) of soil. This will induce new roots to grow from the base of each leaf joint along the stem, to form a network of additional nutrient providers for the developing marrow.

Laterals (side shoots) will grow from each side of the main growing stem, and their growing tips should be pinched out when they reach the limits of the plant's growing area. Sub-laterals should be cut off as they appear.

When the main growing stem has reached the end of its 10ft (3m) allotted area, it should be trained back towards the main root. The original laterals can be removed from the side of the plant when the main growing tip is on the return journey. This will allow you to keep on burying the main runner as it grows. The reason why we allow some of these laterals to partly develop is so that their leaf covering area can assist the plant to develop and prosper. If they were left untrimmed, then I can assure you that you will end up with a massive plant but no record-breaking marrows.

The growing stem of a marrow plant will be very thick and heavy, but although the stalk may have to lift it 6in (15cm) or more above the ground as the marrow grows, the marrow, unlike a pumpkin, will not suffer stress cracks as a result.

Pollination

The female flowers on marrow plants grown outdoors will probably be pollinated by bees,

A marrow plant should be transplanted to its permanent home when it has six leaves; this raised bed has been filled with a mixture of 75 per cent peat and 25 per cent soil to encourage strong roots to develop.

insects and sometimes the wind, but I prefer to avert the risk of failure by hand pollinating.

A marrow plant is capable of supporting three giant specimens, and although many more female flowers will form, you must choose three along the main growing stem for pollination; any small marrows which develop on the plant's laterals or sub-laterals through natural pollination should be removed to the kitchen when they reach approximately 9in (23cm) in length.

A female flower will have a small marrow behind the petals, while a male one has only a stem (see page 85). First cut a male flower from the plant, and carefully remove its petals until only the stamen full of pollen is left. Push the stamen into the centre of a female flower once or twice, then tie a paper or polythene bag over the female flower, to prevent the effects of

marrow chutney

6lb (3kg) prepared marrow
8oz (225g) salt
8oz (225g) onion, peeled and chopped
6 cloves
3 chillies
1 tablespoon turmeric powder
4 tablespoons ground ginger
3 tablespoons mustard
1 pint (600ml) vinegar
1½lb (675g) sugar

1. Cut the marrow into ½in (1cm) cubes, place in a dish and sprinkle with the salt. Leave to stand overnight, then rinse and drain well.
2. Boil the other ingredients together for 10 minutes, then add the marrow and continue boiling for 30 minutes or until the marrow is tender.
3. Put into clean, warm jars.

marrow and ginger jam

5lb (2.25kg) prepared marrow
5lb (2.25kg) sugar
6oz (175g) crystallized ginger
the juice and finely grated rind of 3 lemons

1. Cut the marrow into approximately 1in (2.5cm) cubes.
2. Put the marrow and sugar into your jam pan in layers and leave it covered for 24 hours.
3. Add the crystallized ginger, the lemon rind and juice, then simmer for 3-5 hours, stirring occasionally, until it reaches setting point.
4. Bottle in warm jars.

marrow cream

4lb (1.8kg) prepared marrow
4lb (1.8kg) sugar
8oz (225g) butter
the rind and juice of 3 lemons

1. Cut the marrow into ½in (1cm) cubes, then place them in boiling water and simmer until soft.
2. Beat the softened marrow to a pulp, then add the sugar, butter and finally the lemon rind and juice.
3. Mix well together, then boil for another 10-15 minutes, until the mixture is as clear as honey.
4. Put into clean, warm jars, replace the lids when cool and use as jam.

marrow casserole

3lb (1.5kg) prepared marrow
2oz (50g) butter
3 tablespoons mixed fresh herbs: tarragon, mint, parsley and chives
salt and black pepper

1. Cut the marrow into 1in (2.5cm) slices, then peel and cut them into rough chunks, discarding the seeds.
2. Generously butter an ovenproof dish, then add the marrow with the remaining butter, cut into small knobs, and sprinkle with the herbs. Season with salt and pepper.
3. Cover the dish with a lid or foil and bake in the centre of a preheated oven at 350°F, 180°C, Gas mark 4 until just tender (after about 30 minutes). Do not overcook.
4. Serve the marrow casserole at once, straight from the dish, with plenty of warm, crusty bread.

rainfall or wind from destroying all your work.

The bag should be removed after three days, and the marrow should then start to develop rapidly. It will complete its growing cycle approximately four weeks after pollination, but a marrow can safely be left on the plant to mature for many months.

Feeding

A high nitrogen liquid feed, with a formula of 20N 10P 10K, should be applied to the main roots of the plant once a week from the second week following transplanting, up until the last marrow is harvested. This feed can also be applied along the main growing stem once it has been covered with soil. A twice weekly foliar feed of ⅛ strength will also be beneficial, and should be applied early in the morning so that the leaves have a chance to dry out during the day.

A marrow weighing 108lb 2oz (49kg) was grown in 1990 by Bernard Lavery in Llanharry, South Wales.

Spraying

Giant marrow leaves can grow from 2 to 3ft (60–90cm) in height, and up to 2ft (60cm) across; as they grow very close together, it is almost impossible to spray properly underneath them once they are fully developed.

A spraying programme with a suitable systemic insecticide mixture should be carried out every two weeks, beginning a week after the plants have been transplanted. This early start should allow the plants to build up a resistance to many pests and diseases before the leaves are fully developed and only the tops can be reached by the spray.

To prevent scorch damage to the leaves, spraying should be carried out at the end of the day, and never in direct sunlight.

Harvesting

Harvesting a marrow is very easy, but they can weigh much more than you might imagine. Some varieties have a hollow centre, but others are almost solid. If your's has grown to a massive size, I advise you to seek some assistance in lifting it.

The marrow should be cut from the plant, and any soil clinging to the underneath washed off or removed with a small hand brush. To prevent dehydration, it should then be wrapped up in dry blankets or cloths, and stored in a cool, dry, frost-free place.

The regulations for entry into the record books are that a marrow must be in a sound condition and free from soil, dirt or any other foreign bodies. A maximum of 1in (2.5cm) of stalk can be left on.

A marrow plant can be trained back towards the main roots once the growing tip has reached the limits of its allocated growing area.

Bernard Lavery supports and exhibits his prize-winning marrow.

leeks

Growing giant leeks has a fascination that is difficult to explain. In some parts of the world it quite commonly causes garden warfare among normally reserved and perfectly sensible people.

The leek has a distinctive and very decorative seedhead.

A leek is a hardy biennial and a member of the onion family; their seeds look identical. Leeks are mainly cultivated for the blanched lower part of their leaves, which can be boiled or braised. The green tops can also be used to enhance the flavour of soups, stews and many other cooked dishes. They are a useful winter vegetable, as they have an eight-month harvesting season and can endure even severe frosts.

Some leek-growing areas abound in tales of sabotage and skulduggery, and I have had reports of shot guns, guard dogs and electric fences being used to protect prize specimens from jealous competitors or vandals. However, I have been growing exhibition leeks myself for thirty-five years, and am pleased to be able to report that I have had no such problems to date.

Planning ahead

Gardeners today have a choice of two kinds of leeks: the short thick-shafted 'Pot' varieties, or the 'Blanch' varieties with a much thinner shaft, which may grow up to 4ft (1.2m) long.

Although the 'Blanch' varieties are the ones most commonly grown worldwide, the 'Pot' leek with its shorter, stocky shaft and very wide fleshy green leaves (flags), weigh much heavier, and these are the ones I attempt to grow to a giant size.

Each pot leek plant will require a 3ft (90cm) square growing area, and although the roots will not penetrate deeply into the ground, well cultivated soil with a high proportion of humus mixed into it will provide the free drainage that is essential for success.

Seeds

Pot leek seeds can be purchased from seed merchants in most countries of the world, but it will be best if you can find a specialist grower to supply you. Their strains of leek are usually far superior to the ones sold in garden suppliers or general stores.

You can also sometimes buy pot leek 'pips', which resemble miniature onion sets; these form on the seedheads, between the seed stalks, and are harvested with the seed and dried out and stored until it is time to replant

leek pie

4 bacon rashers
1½lb (675g) leeks
¼ pint (150ml) milk
¼ pint (150ml) single cream
2 eggs
salt and pepper to taste
8oz (225g) shortcrust pastry

1. *Grill the bacon rashers, then chop them into small pieces.*
2. *Wash the leeks thoroughly and cut them into 1in (2.5cm) lengths. Boil in salted water for 8-10 minutes or until soft.*
3. *Beat the milk, cream and eggs together, season, then pour over the leeks.*
4. *Roll out the pastry and cover the filling: make a slit in the top to allow the steam to escape during cooking. Brush the top with a little egg wash to glaze.*
5. *Bake in the centre of a preheated hot oven at 425°F, 200°C, Gas mark 7 for 20 minutes, then reduce the heat to very moderate (325°F, 160°C, Gas mark 3) for a further 20 minutes. The reduction of heat ensures that the savoury filling does not become overheated and curdle.*

leeks lucullus

4 large leeks, cleaned, trimmed and chopped
8 medium-sized potatoes, peeled
¼ pint (150ml) single cream
4oz (115g) butter or margarine
5oz (150g) cheese, grated
salt and pepper
8 bacon rashers, rinded and grilled

1. *Cook the leeks and potatoes in separate pans of boiling salted water until tender. Drain well, then rub through a sieve.*

2. *Beat the cream into the purée, then add the butter or margarine, 4oz (115g) cheese and pepper. Turn the mixture into a shallow flameproof serving dish.*
3. *Sprinkle over the remaining cheese and brown under the grill. Serve garnished with the bacon, cut into pieces.*

cock-a-leekie soup

a 3lb(1.5kg) boiling chicken
8 prunes
6 peppercorns
1 tablespoon salt
1 giant leek
finely chopped parsley
to garnish

1. *Soak the prunes for 6 hours in cold water.*
2. *Wipe the trussed chicken, rinse the giblets and place both in a saucepan. Pour over cold water to cover. Add peppercorns and salt and bring to the boil.*
3. *Remove scum from the surface, cover with a tight-fitting lid and simmer for about 1½ hours.*
4. *Trim the coarse outer leaves off the leek to within 2in (5cm) of the top of the white stem and cut off the roots. Split the leek lengthways, wash well under cold water, then cut into 1in (2.5cm) pieces.*
5. *Skim the soup again before adding the leeks and the prunes, then simmer for another 30 minutes.*
6. *Lift the chicken and giblets from the soup; remove the skin and bones from the chicken flesh, discard them and cut the meat into small pieces.*
7. *Add the chicken pieces to the soup and season if needed. Just before serving the hot soup, sprinkle over the finely chopped parsley.*

them in mid-winter. Each seedhead will produce 20–30 pips, and the difference between a leek seed and a leek pip is that whereas two parents are needed to form a seed, only one parent is required for a pip. A pip is therefore similar to a cutting, and will produce identical specimens to the parent; with a little extra care and attention, it may even produce better ones.

Bernard carries out a weekly inspection of his leeks, checking for any signs of pests or disease.

Sowing the seeds

The first sowing should be made in mid-winter, and a second one as a back-up a few weeks later. Allow thirty to thirty-six weeks to harvest. The seeds should be sown ½in (12mm) deep in a tray of a peat-based compost, before being

A selection of giant leeks in pristine condition at a giant vegetable contest.

each plant will be unnecessary. If, however, they are intended for the kitchen, each base should be surrounded with a 6in (15cm) strip of cardboard secured with string or cord. As the shaft thickens, the ties must be slackened to prevent any damage to the plant.

Feeding
A weekly high nitrogen liquid feed, with a formula of 20N 10P 10K, should be used throughout the growing season, and an

watered and placed in a propagator with a heat setting of 70° F (21° C). They will take fourteen to twenty days to germinate, and as soon as this occurs the tray should be moved into a position of full daylight at a minimum temperature of 60° F (15° C).

Transplanting
When the leek plants have grown to approximately 5in (12cm) high, they should be transplanted into their permanent growing position. A circle of canes should be pushed into the soil 2ft (60cm) from the plant, and string tied horizontally around them at 6in (15cm) intervals. As the leek plants grow, their heavy leaves will be supported by these strings, and this will prevent them drooping towards the ground and eventually splitting.

A leek weighing 12lb 2oz (5.45kg) was grown in 1987 by Mr P. Harrigan in Linton, Northumberland.

If you are growing leeks for a show, or in an attempt to break a record, blanching the base of

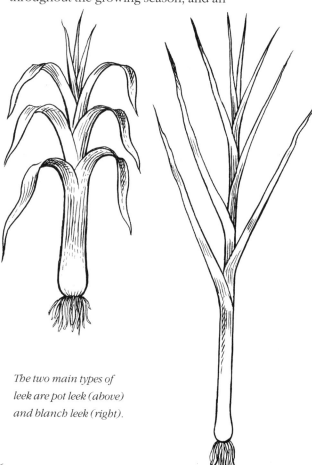

The two main types of leek are pot leek (above) and blanch leek (right).

additional mid-week foliar feed of a ¼ strength mixture will be beneficial. A little 'spreader', or a drop of washing-up liquid mixed with the foliar feed will help the spray to stick to the leaves.

Spraying

A complete spraying programme of a systemic insecticide and fungicide should be carried out every two weeks throughout the growing season, and once again a 'spreader' should be mixed with the spraying mixture to prevent it rolling off the leaves.

The spray should be applied to both sides of the leaves, and the chemicals will gradually be absorbed, to enable the plant to build up a resistance to many potential pests and diseases.

Harvesting

Great care must be taken when harvesting leeks, as their tender leaves are easily damaged. Before you attempt to dig the roots from the soil, the foliage must be tied securely together. This is a four-handed job, and I always invite one of my friends to help.

The first pair of hands will be needed to hold the leaves together vertically, while the other person ties pieces of thick string or cord around them at 6in (15cm) intervals, starting from the bottom. Then, while one person holds up the pillar of leaves, the other should carefully dig the roots out with a garden fork.

Once out of the earth, the roots should be cleaned of soil, using a hosepipe with a medium strength flow of water. As the roots may be left on the plant, and will contribute to the final weight of the leek, great care and patience must be exercised. To keep a leek plant looking fresh and healthy, and to prevent it from losing weight, stand it in a bucket of water.

The regulations for entry into the record books are that a leek must be in a sound condition and be free from dirt, sticks or stones, or any foreign bodies.

LEEK HAZARDS

RUST is undoubtedly the leek's greatest enemy. The airborne spores will travel for miles, and can devastate a whole leek bed in a matter of a few weeks if not checked. The disease can be identified by small dark brown spots appearing on the undersides of the leaves. If these are not immediately treated, they will spread rapidly to cover the entire leek plant.

A suitable systemic fungicide should be sprayed every seven days on to all parts of an infected plant until all visible signs of the disease have been eliminated. Any heavily infected plants should be relegated to the dustbin.

WHITE TOP is a common leek disease and starts with the tips of the leaves turning white and papery. This will soon spread downwards and cause blotches to all parts of the leaves. White Top will stunt the plant's growth and end any aspirations you may have had of growing a giant leek. However, your regular spraying programme should do much to deter the disease.

LEEK MOTH becomes active in mid- or late spring, the female laying its eggs on the plant at or near ground-level. The resulting grey caterpillars will bore into the upper surfaces of the leaves, causing elongated white streaks. These streaks will eventually turn into holes, and soon the whole plant will be ruined. To deter this pest, make sure that you spray the soil at the base of the plants during your regular spraying programme.

chapter thirteen

swedes

Swedes belong to the brassica family; they are most closely related to turnips, although their globular roots will grow to a much larger size.

Swedes grow very quickly, and the timescale from seed sowing to harvesting may be as little as twelve weeks. If they are harvested in the late autumn, the tops should be removed and the roots stored in boxes of dried peat or sand.

Swedes are a useful winter vegetable when other vegetables are scarce. The outside skins of swede roots are often purple, while the flesh inside varies from light yellow to orange. The flesh is usually boiled and then mashed with a little butter and seasoning. They may also be diced into 1in (2.5cm) cubes and used in stews, casseroles and soups.

Planning ahead

The method used for growing giant swedes differs slightly from the normal one, but the finished product will be just as tasty, and will certainly feed more people.

Swedes need maximum ventilation plus uninterrupted sunlight, so they prefer south-facing ground in the most exposed part of the garden. They require deeply cultivated soil with plenty of humus, and a pH of 6.5–7. Soil that has had fresh farmyard manure dug in, or that is too rich in nitrogen from last year's manure or feeds, will tend to induce rot, and may also make the

swedes run prematurely to seed. The method I use is to make ridges of soil 12in (30cm) high, similar to those used for potatoes. A space of at least 3ft (90cm) should be allowed between the top of one ridge and the top of the next one. Alternatively they can be grown in raised beds.

Seeds

Although ordinary seeds will be readily available at any garden store, you may have to search through seed catalogues or gardening publications to find seed for growing giants.

During Punky Night, *a festival held around the time of Hallowe'en at Hinton St. George, Somerset, England, lanterns are made from hollowed-out mangel-wurzels, or swedes, and carried as a deterrent to evil spirits.*

Seeds of giant swedes are sown in groups of six, ½ in (12mm) deep,
on top of a 12in (30cm) high ridge of soil that has been enriched with
generous quantities of organic matter.

Sowing the seeds

The timescale from seed sowing to harvesting a fully developed swede is approximately twenty weeks, and the first sowing should not be earlier than the beginning of summer.

Sow groups of six seeds closely together, ½in (12mm) deep, every 3ft (90cm) along the top of each ridge, and then water lightly. The seeds should germinate in five or six days.

Growing on

When the seedlings have reached a height of about 6in (15cm), each group of plants should be thinned out to leave only the strongest one. This should be carried out in the late evening.

The ridge of soil should then be pared away little by little from the remaining swede, until only the bottom tip of the root remains in the soil. This is to induce the root to reach down further in search of nutrients, and if the root is exceptionally strong and vigorous, you may find that the ridge of soil has been almost levelled by the time this important operation is completed.

A swede weighing 53lb 8oz (24.07kg) was grown in 1993 by Mr P. Lillie, in Uxbridge, Ontario, Canada.

Your giant swedes may look half dead by the end of it, but do not despair; by the next morning they will have started to recover, and at the end of the season you will find that the swede roots which were exposed at this early stage have developed below the ground as well as above. You should certainly finish up with huge swedes.

Feeding

To encourage a swede root to develop below ground, do not give additional liquid feeds to the plants for at least four weeks after being thinned out. From then on, a balanced liquid feed with a formula of 10N 10P 10K can be applied to the whole area. In extremely hot weather conditions, a 2in (5cm) thick mulch of peat should be applied to the soil surrounding each plant, to protect its hundreds of tiny

SWEDE HAZARDS

FLEA BEETLE can attack the leaves of a swede plant from the very first day the leaves appear above the soil. Damage is usually identified by new holes appearing daily in the centre of the leaves. The beetles are difficult to catch, as they jump when disturbed. Appropriate insecticides should always be included in your spraying programme.

CATERPILLARS devour the flesh of the leaves, gretly reducing the plant's vigour and preventing it from reaching its full potential. Butterflies often lay their clutches of small yellow eggs on the undersides of the leaves, and if these eggs are not removed or destroyed, caterpillars will soon hatch out.

Your regular spraying programme of a systemic insecticide mixture will deter butterflies and destroy caterpillars, but a more frequent application will be required if an infestation occurs.

POWDERY MILDEW usually develops when there is poor air circulation, but it can also occur during damp, misty or cold weather conditions. It is identified by a white powdery film covering the upper surfaces of a plant's leaves. A systemic fungicide spray will eliminate the disease if it is treated early.

SLUGS are very partial to a feed of fresh young swede leaves, and a few slug pellets should be sprinkled around the base of each plant at regular intervals throughout the season.

Above: *Young swede plants are growing in a raised bed; they will be thinned out to leave only the strongest one in each bed when they reach a height of 6in (15cm).*

Left: *This newly harvested swede is being washed with a medium-strength flow of water from a hosepipe.*

surface roots from damage. This mulch should be watered daily in addition to the weekly feed.

Spraying

A full spraying programme should be carried out every two weeks from as soon as the seeds have germinated until harvesting. Use a systemic insecticide and fungicide mixture, which will help the swedes build up a resistance to pests and diseases.

Harvesting

Before harvesting a giant swede, it is advisable to snap off some of the large outside leaves.

A healthy giant swede plant should be developing its root below the ground as well as on top of it.

Then hold up the remaining foliage and use a garden fork to dig up the root. Great care must be taken to prevent any small side roots from breaking away, as they will each add a little to the swede's final weight.

When the plant has been dislodged from the ground, hose down the roots with a medium strength flow of water to remove any remaining soil. The remaining foliage should be left on the plant until the last possible moment before it is weighed, to prevent dehydration.

The regulations for entry into the record books are that a swede should be in a sound condition, and free from dirt, sticks or stones and any other foreign bodies. Its foliage should be cut off as near to the main body as possible.

swede wine

This makes a dry white wine which improves with keeping.

*4½lb (2kg) swedes
2lb 4oz (1.2kg) sugar
1oz (25g) bruised root ginger
9 pints (5 litres) water
yeast and nutrients for winemaking*

*1. Scrub and clean the swede well, then chop it up into chunks.
2. Boil with the ginger in 7 pints (4 litres) of water for 1½ hours. Add the sugar and boil for a further 45 minutes.
3. Boil the rest of the water and add it, then allow the mixture to cool. When it is tepid, pour into demijohns or wine casks.
4. Add the yeast and nutrient and fit the air lock. Leave for at least three months, then syphon into fresh demijohns or bottles.*

chapter fourteen

runner beans

Although the early varieties of runner bean plants were vigorous climbers, the actual beans were only about 5in (12cm) long. After years of selection and cross-breeding, some varieties will now produce beans over 20in (50cm) long.

Runner beans were introduced to Europe from South America in the mid-seventeenth century. They are now grown worldwide in vast quantities, the long pods usually chopped or sliced before being boiled and served as a vegetable with a cooked meal. In some areas runner beans are grown for the bean seeds inside the pods, which are used in salads, casseroles and stews as well as in many other dishes.

Beans should be grown outdoors, and if you intend to grow the world's longest bean, I advise growing ten plants well away from those to be grown for table use. The reason for this is that once one bean is allowed to mature and form seeds inside it, the plant will think that its work for the season has been completed. Any further beans which develop on the plant will only grow to half their potential length and their texture will be tough and stringy. These 'giants' will be edible but, like all runner beans, if you wish to eat the pods, they should be harvested befor the beans inside form.

A runner bean measuring 48in (121.9cm) was grown in 1994 by Mr Gordon Rogerson, in Robertsville, North Carolina, U.S.A.

Soil preparation

The underlying soil for any runner beans should be deeply dug in the autumn, and have plenty of humus or peat incorporated into it. To grow giants, I find the best way is then to dig a trench 12ft (3.6m) long, 18in (45cm) wide and 12in (30cm) deep and, in order to retain moisture in hot summer weather, to line the bottom 2in (5cm) with folded newspapers, filling the remainder with a 50/50 mixture of peat and soil.

This should then be covered with a sprinkling of 8oz (225g) of lime, and left to overwinter. The ideal pH level for beans is 6.8, and the growing mixture should be checked at

Beans grown for length are being thoroughly inspected at a horticultural show for giant vegetables.

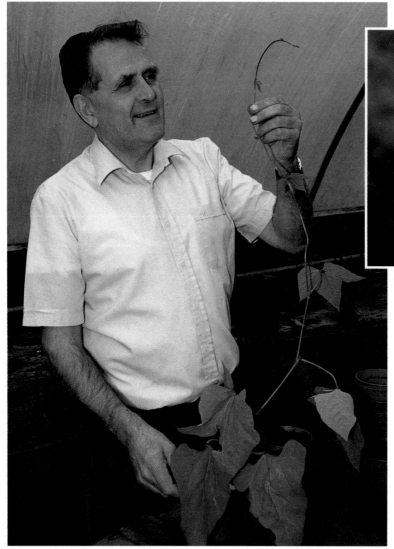

A bean plant is trained to grow anti-clockwise up its supporting pole.

A young bean plant is all ready to be transplanted into its permanent growing position.

the beginning of spring, and either increased by adding lime, or lowered by adding humus or sedge peat.

Supporting the canes

Two 5ft (1.5m) stakes should be driven into the ground in the corners at either end of one side of the trench; wires will be attached to these stakes which will in turn support the canes up which the bean plants will be grown.

When the spring arrives and weather conditions allow you to work in the garden, the canes must be secured in position so that everything is ready and waiting for the young plants once they are ready.

First lay a plank of wood on the soil on the opposite side of the trench to the two stakes. This will enable you to walk up and down the row of beans throughout the season without compacting the soil. Next, secure a length of sturdy galvanized wire 4ft (120cm) high as tightly as possible between the two stakes. Then lean ten 8ft (2.5m) long canes against the wire at an angle, and push their bottom ends into the soil at the edge of the trench nearest to the plank. These should be spaced at 1ft (30cm) intervals, beginning 1ft (30cm) from the end of the trench. Finally, tie each cane tightly to the horizontal wire with pieces of string.

Seeds

Selecting the correct variety of seeds is obviously important, and once again I suggest that you find a specialist grower to supply you with some of his or her own giant strain.

Sowing the seeds

To cover the risk of poor germination, I always sow twice as many seeds as the number of plants required. They should be sown in late spring, 1in (2.5cm) deep, in 4in (10cm) pots containing peat-based compost, and thoroughly watered before being placed on the glasshouse bench in full daylight. The timescale from sowing seeds to harvesting your beans will be from twenty-two to thirty-two weeks.

Transplanting

Germination should take place in eight to ten days, and once the plants have grown to 4in or 5in (10–12cm) and have developed two strong-looking leaves, they can be set out in their permanent growing positions, 1ft (30cm) apart, under a cane and in the centre of the prepared trench.

Growing on

As soon as a plant is tall enough, it should be secured to its cane and trained to grow up it in an anti-clockwise direction. Plastic or string ties should be used as additional support at intervals of 9in (23cm).

RUNNER BEAN HAZARDS

SLUGS can cause damage to the leaves of young bean plants, and will often eat holes in the actual beans if these are allowed to touch the ground. A regular sprinkling of slug pellets on the soil surrounding the plants should help to keep these creatures at bay.

WOODLICE will attack the stems of young bean plants at soil level, eating their way more than halfway through the stems and rendering them useless. To deter these night time invaders, sprinkle a little insecticide powder regularly on the soil near each plant, starting as soon as they have been transplanted.

BLACK FLY will take up residence on the underside of a bean plant's leaves, and an infestation of these tiny pests can often go undetected for weeks, by which time the plants will have lost a lot of their vigour. To eliminate black fly, apply a suitable insecticide spray to both sides of the infected leaves, and repeat seven days later. This again should be carried out in the late evening.

BEAN WEEVILS will attack the leaves of young bean plants by eating U-shaped notches around the edges. This will dramatically reduce the plant's performance, but once these small beetles have been eliminated with a suitable insecticide spray, the plant should make a full recovery.

The most successful way of pollinating the female flowers is by hand, using a fine paintbrush.

creamy beans with carrots

*1lb (450g) runner beans,
stringed and sliced
8oz (225g) young carrots, sliced
salt and pepper
2 tablespoons oil
1 tablespoon chopped fresh mint
3 tablespoons fresh or soured cream*

*1. Put the carrots into a saucepan with salt
and pepper and add enough water to cover.
Bring to the boil, cover and simmer for 5
minutes.
2. Drain off a little of the water, then add
the beans and oil. Mix well, bring back to
the boil and re-cover the pan.*

*3. Simmer for a further 10-12 minutes or
until the vegetables are tender. Drain off the
liquid and stir in the mint and cream.*

runner beans with cream

*2lb (900g) runner beans,
stringed and sliced
4 tablespoons single cream or top of milk*

*1. Cook the beans in boiling salted water
until they are just tender. Drain well and
turn into a heated ovenproof serving dish.
2. Stir in the cream and warm in a preheated moderate oven (350°F, 180°C, Gas
mark 4) for a few minutes before serving.*

The growing tips of the laterals (side shoots) should be pinched out once the first leaf has developed, and the sub-laterals which grow from that one leaf joint allowed to grow until they develop a truss of flowers. Their growing tips should then also be removed, as should that of the main runner when it reaches the top of its supporting cane.

When all the beans have set on a truss and are approximately 4in (10cm) long, all the weaker ones should be cut off, leaving only the two strongest to grow on.

If the end of a bean touches a leaf, it will probably try to curve around it, but with the supporting canes leaning at an angle, the majority should be free to hang down and grow unobstructed, leaving you at the end of the season with long straight beans.

Pollination

Since you are severely limiting the number of bean-bearing trusses the plant produces, I advise you to hand-pollinate to ensure that the flowers carried on these trusses are successfully pollinated. For this

*The supporting system of stakes, wire and
canes held at an angle allows the beans to
hang freely, ensuring that they will grow as
straight as possible.*

you will need a very small pencil-like paintbrush and a little patience.

First squeeze the back of a flower with your index finger and thumb until the front opens up. In the open mouth of the flower you should see a small, light green stamen, full of pollen, on the left of the centre. Touch this gently with the brush, and go from flower to flower, and back to the first one, brushing against the stigmas as you go, until all the flowers which require pollinating have been visited. In this way, minute particles of pollen will be transferred from the stamen of one bean flower to the stigma of the next.

Feeding

A high nitrogen liquid feed with a compound formula of 20N 10P 10K should be applied to the roots of your bean plants every two weeks as soon as the plants have climbed half way up their canes.

A twice weekly foliar feed of ⅛ strength will also be beneficial, and a daily liberal watering along the length of the trench will ensure that the roots do not dry out.

Spraying

A spraying programme with a suitable insecticide and fungicide mixture should be carried out every two weeks throughout the growing season. This should be done in the late evening when the bees are no longer active.

Harvesting

Harvesting a bean is easy: you just snip the stalk from the plant with a pair of scissors. It is also quite simple to straighten a bent bean after harvesting. The bean should be gently tied as straight as possible, with pieces of string or cord at 3in (7cm) intervals, to a length of cane or

A healthy looking truss of giant beans hangs among the dense foliage.

strip of wood. The whole assembly should then be wrapped up in a damp towel and left for twenty-four hours. By that time the bean will have become more supple and the ties can be adjusted to draw it completely straight.

The regulations for entry into the record books are that a bean must be in a sound condition and must be measured in a straight line from end to end. The stalk must not be included in these measurements.

chapter fifteen

parsnips for weight

Parsnips are hardy biennials, natives of Siberia and Europe, and cultivated since Roman times for their bulky, edible roots.

Parsnip roots vary in colour from white to mid-yellow, and contain high quantities of sugar and starch. They are a useful winter vegetable and can be boiled, braised, fried or roasted; they are also ideal subjects for wine-making.

Giant parsnips will taste just as good as ordinary ones and, as their taste improves with age, can be allowed to develop their full potential before being harvested.

Planning ahead

To grow giant parsnips you need a long growing season, poor, well drained soil, and the correct variety of seeds. Parsnips prefer a deep, well cultivated, sandy type soil and, unlike carrots, will not prosper in rich, freshly manured conditions. I recommend that you use raised beds, the higher the better, to grow heavyweight parsnips. Ideal are 45 gallon (200 litre) drums with the top and bottom removed, placed on top of well cultivated soil. They should be filled up in the autumn with a mixture of one-third sand, one-third peat and one-third poor soil, then left to settle until the new year.

A parsnip measuring 171¾in (436.8cm) was grown in 1990 by Bernard Lavery in Llanharry, South Wales.

The pH level can vary greatly when you create these conditions, and I have had excellent results with readings which vary from 5 to 6.5.

Seeds

Always select a variety of parsnip seed that has the potential to grow long and heavy. An old-fashioned open-pollinated type will be far better than a modern F1 hybrid. One parsnip plant will yield anything from 30,000 to 50,000 seeds, and the size of the seeds in a packet will vary from very small ones to others that are twice as big.

When you arrive home, empty the packet of seeds on to the table and grade the seeds into three different sizes: the biggest for growing giants, medium-sized ones as a back-up sowing, and the smallest ones for the kitchen garden.

Parsnips should always be harvested with great care, to keep their side roots intact.

Sowing the seeds

The first sowing of seeds for growing giant parsnips should be made in mid-winter, but two weeks before this the raised beds should be watered and covered with plastic sheets to raise the growing mixture's temperature a little.

PARSNIP HAZARDS

CELERY ROOT FLY can devastate a crop of parsnips by laying their tiny eggs alongside the roots, just below the surface of the soil or growing mixture. The maggots will burrow into the parsnip roots and travel from one end to the other, leaving trails of small dark brown tunnels. This will completely ruin the root and it will very soon begin to rot. Sprinkle insecticide powder on the soil round the roots every two weeks.

CANKER is a common disease to attack parsnips. It is identified by dark brown patches forming on the shoulders of the roots, and is caused by the soil or growing mixture being too rich in itself, or having too much composted manure incorporated into it.

There is no cure for canker, and the roots should be harvested immediately the disease is identified. The infected tops should be be cut off and discarded; there is no reason why the remainder of the root cannot be used in the kitchen.

LEAF MINERS will burrow into the leaf tissues and cause blisters to form. They can be destroyed by squashing them between your fingers, or otherwise by spraying both sides of the leaves with a suitable insecticide mixture.

BLACK FLY are usually found on the undersides of the leaves of parsnips. Plants should be inspected regularly and any infestations sprayed with a suitable insecticide immediately the black fly are detected.

Scatter six seeds per drum on the growing mixture's surface, water them in, then place the polythene sheet back on top and tie it down.

The seeds will take approximately four weeks to germinate at this time of the year, and will sometimes fail altogether. I advise making a back-up sowing of about 100 seeds in a 6in (15cm) plant pot containing peat-based compost at the same time, and putting it in a cold glasshouse. The timescale from seeds to harvested plants is thirty-six to forty weeks.

Growing on

As soon as the surface-sown seedlings have germinated, remove the polythene covers; parsnip seedlings are hardy and will stand even the severest of frosts. They should be thinned out when they have reached 3in (7cm), and only the strongest seedling left to grow on.

Every time the surface of the growing mixture is disturbed by thinning out or weeding, sprinkle a little insecticide powder over it to deter unwelcome pests.

Transplanting

Pot-grown seedlings can be transplanted to other raised beds or used to replace already sown seeds which have failed. The reason for surface sowing and transplanting is to induce the plant to develop more than one root. The more roots that a specimen has, the heavier it should weigh at the end of the season. This is the method to use if you are trying to break a record for the heaviest parsnip. The resulting roots may look unattractive to some people, who will prefer to grow the traditionally shaped parsnips.

Pot-grown seedlings should be transplanted into their permanent growing positions as soon as they have grown to approximately 4in (10cm). Push a thick stick or broom handle into the growing mixture to make a hole for the seedling's tap root. When the root has been inserted, fill the hole by pouring water on to the growing mixture's surface, washing it into the hole until it is full. Transplanted seedlings will need watering every day until you are absolutely certain that the operation has been successful.

Feeding

Daily watering will be required throughout the whole season for parsnips in raised beds. They

creamed parsnips

1½lb (675g) parsnips, peeled and diced
salt and pepper
1 pint (600ml) milk
2oz (50g) butter
2 tablespoons chopped parsley

1. Put all the parsnips in a saucepan
with the well seasoned milk. Cover the pan
and simmer steadily until nearly tender.
2. Remove the lid to allow any excess
liquid to evaporate and stir several times
during this stage to prevent the
parsnips sticking to the pan.
3. Blend in the butter and chopped parsley
just before serving.

beef and parsnip pie

1 tablespoon beef dripping
1 large onion (2lb/900g), peeled
and chopped
1 garlic clove, crushed
1½lb (675g) minced beef

2 tablespoons flour
8oz (225g) canned tomatoes
7fl oz (200ml) beef stock
salt and pepper
1 teaspoon dried basil or marjoram
10oz (275g) potatoes, peeled,
cooked and mashed
1½lb (675g) parsnips, peeled,
cooked and mashed
3oz (75g) butter

1. Melt the dripping in a saucepan
and fry the onion and garlic until softened.
Add the beef and fry for 10 minutes or
until browned.
2. Stir in the flour, then add tomatoes,
stock, salt, pepper and herbs.
Bring to the boil, cover and simmer for
15-20 minutes, then turn the beef mixture
into a baking dish.
3. Mix together the mashed potatoes
and parsnips and add butter, salt and
pepper. Beat well, then spread or pipe over
the top of the beef mixture.
4. Bake in a preheated moderately
hot oven (400°F, 200°C, Gas mark 6)
for 25-30 minutes or until the top
is beginning to brown.

will also appreciate a balanced liquid feed with a compound formula of 10N 10P 10K every third week, starting from the beginning of the summer season.

A balanced foliar feed of ⅛ strength will also benefit the plants, and should be applied in the evenings from mid-summer onwards. Provide a 2in (5cm) thick surface mulch of moss peat to conserve moisture if the weather conditions are exceptionally hot.

Harvesting
Extreme care must be taken when harvesting giant parsnips. There may be dozens of small side roots attached to the main root, and every effort must be made to keep these side roots intact as the plant is removed.

The growing mixture should be scraped away from the roots, little by little, until the whole rooting system can be lifted without being damaged. Hose the roots down with a medium strength water flow to remove any clinging soil or dirt. To prevent dehydration, the foliage should not be removed until the last possible moment before the parsnips are weighed.

The regulations for entry into the record books are that a parsnip must be in a sound condition and free from soil, dirt or any foreign bodies. The foliage of parsnips must be cut off as near to the top of the root's shoulders as possible.

chapter sixteen

beetroot

The many different kinds of beet all derive from the wild slender perennial Beta vulgaris, *which was grown in Roman times along the coastal regions of western Europe, the Mediterranean and eastward as far as India.*

Today's farmers grow mangel-wurzels as a stock feed, and sugar beet, which now supplements sugar cane to provide most of the world's sugar. Modern-day gardeners, however, grow many different kinds of beet for table use. These include seakale beet and spinach beet for their edible leaves, and red beetroot for their roots.

For the record books, the beetroot counts as a class on its own. Beetroot are mostly grown for use in salad, when the roots are boiled and sliced; but they can also be pickled, frozen or stored in dry sand, and can be eaten hot or cold at any time of the year. They provide a useful ingredient in chutney and wine-making as well as a basis for soup. The leaves of young beetroot can also be eaten as 'greens'.

As most gardeners prefer to harvest their beetroot when they are small, sweet and sometimes only half developed, growing huge beetroot may not appeal to them at first. However, most of the giant varieties have exactly the same qualities as ordinary ones. I always sow seeds a little closer than I need, to enable me to harvest some of the young beetroot for the kitchen as I thin out the plants. The few that I

leave in the ground to grow on into real giants are usually given eventually to one of my wine-making neighbours.

Soil preparation

Beetroot should be grown outdoors, and the soil should be deeply cultivated in the autumn, with plenty of humus or peat incorporated into it. I do not advise the use of fresh farmyard manure and, as too much lime will cause warts and canker to form on the roots, aim to keep the pH level below 6.

When spring arrives the soil should be raked into ridged rows 1ft (30cm) high and 2ft (60cm) apart. The total length of these ridges will determine how many giant beetroots you will be able to grow; each plant will eventually need a 3ft (90cm) spacing.

Beetroot plants should be thinned out to leave the two strongest when they are about 2in (5cm) in high.

BEETROOT HAZARDS

HEART ROT is identified by the leaves wilting in the summer heat. The tops of the roots will also have dark brown patches similar to the canker which sometimes attacks parsnips. If your plants are showing these symptoms, the root centres will almost certainly have started to rot. Infected plants should be relegated to the dustbin. The problem is caused by a Boron deficiency, or by over-limed soil.

BOLTING, or throwing seed, may occur in the first year if beetroots suffer a check at any time, when they will develop a hard core and become inedible. Beetroots are biennials, so they should go to seed only in their second year. The main causes of a plant being checked are if the seed is sown too early, if the soil dries out, if there is a shortage of organic matter, or if the plants are thinned out too late.

WOODLICE and **SLUGS** Woodlice will attack the seedlings when they are very small. Slugs will attack the leaves at any time, and will also bore holes into the roots when they begin to swell. To deter these two unwanted visitors, seedlings should be dusted with an insecticide powder, when the leaves are dry, as soon as germination occurs, and a few slug pellets should be sprinkled around the plants every few weeks.

Seeds

When selecting seeds for growing giant beetroots, you should search seed catalogues and stores to find a variety which has the genetic capabilities to grow big specimens. The timescale from sowing beetroot seeds to harvesting edible thinnings is only about three months, but to grow them on to full maturity a minimum of four months should be allowed.

Once the beetroot roots have started to swell, they should be thinned out to a single one per raised bed.

Beetroots can be left in the ground for several months without going to seed (bolting), provided that the seed was not sown too early in the year.

Sowing the seeds

Sow the seed in late spring, in groups of three seeds, ½in (12mm) deep and 1ft (30cm) apart, on top of the prepared ridges. Water the whole length of the ridges lightly, and keep them moist until the seeds have germinated, which should take between ten and twelve days.

Growing on

You will find that ten or more seedlings come up where only three were planted. The reason for this is that each seed is made up of a cluster of smaller ones. There are single-celled varieties now available, but these varieties rarely grow to a huge size.

When the seedlings have grown to a height of approximately 2in (5cm), they should be thinned out to leave only the two strongest. When these two remaining plants reach a height of 5–6in (12–15cm), carefully scratch the soil of the ridges away from the roots until the ground is level. At this point only the tips of the roots will be in the soil, and the remainder of the plant will be lying on the ground looking

A beetroot weighing 40lb 8oz (18.2kg) was grown in 1994 by Ian Neale in Newport, South Wales.

half-dead. Lightly water the whole area and sprinkle it with slug pellets. This task, which will induce the roots to work harder to save the plant and therefore grow much stronger and bigger, should be undertaken in the late evening to avoid putting the plants under additional heat stress. By the next morning they will have started to recover.

Once the beetroot roots have started to swell visibly, it is time to thin them out once more, leaving one plant every 3ft (90cm). These thinnings can be used for the table and, although they will be larger than those you are accustomed to eating, they should nevertheless be very tasty.

Feeding
A balanced liquid feed with a compound formula of 10N 10P 10K can be applied to the soil from mid-summer right up until harvest time. An ⅛ strength foliar feed will also be beneficial to the plants from around this time onwards.

Spraying
Beetroot plants should be given a suitable spraying programme every two weeks from when the seedlings are first thinned out, and this should continue throughout the entire growing season.

Harvesting
Before you begin to harvest a heavy beetroot, it is as well to break off a few of the big, heavy, outside leaves. The roots should then be dug out of the soil with a garden fork, making sure that none of the smaller tap roots is broken off. These will all count when the beetroot plant is finally weighed. To prevent dehydration, cut off the remaining foliage at the last possible moment before the specimen is weighed.

beetroot beer

1lb (450g) beetroot
8oz (225g) sugar
1 pint (600ml) stout

1. Wash the beetroot and slice into a bowl. Sprinkle on the sugar and leave for 24 hours.
2. Strain, then add the stout. Bottle and cork. The beer will be ready to drink in 7 to 14 days.

beetroot chutney

3lb (1.5kg) prepared beetroot
1lb (450g) mixed dried fruit
8oz (225g) onions, peeled and chopped
1 pint (600ml) vinegar
8oz (225g) sugar
1 tablespoon salt
1 teaspoon pepper
1oz (25g) allspice

1. Wash and trim the beetroot and cook it in salted water until tender. Skin carefully and chop into small pieces. (4-5lb/1.8-2.25kg raw beetroot will be required to obtain 3lb/1.5kg prepared weight.)
2. Chop the fruit and onions finely and add to the vinegar with the sugar, salt, pepper and allspice.
3. Boil until tender and the mixture is beginning to thicken. Add the chopped beetroot and boil gently for 15 minutes.

To qualify for entry into the record books, a beetroot must be in a sound condition and free from dirt or soil and any foreign bodies. The foliage must be cut off as near to the main body of the root as possible.

chapter seventeen

water melons

*Water melons are grown in many regions of the world.
In hotter climates they will grow to huge proportions in open
fields or gardens; in cooler ones they are best grown
under glass or polythene.*

The outer skins of water melons vary in colour from light green to black, and the inside flesh from light yellow to a deep purple. They are commonly used as a starter course to a meal, or as a refreshing chilled snack. They are extremely low in calories and therefore an ideal subject for use in diets.

Although a water melon is a fruit, for horticultural judging purposes it is always classified as a vegetable.

Soil preparation

A deeply cultivated soil with plenty of humus incorporated into it, and with a pH of 6.5, will provide ideal conditions for giant water melons. Transplanted plants thrive in loose soil, and I advise preparing their growing areas in late spring, so that the soil does not compact. Each plant will need a cultivated area of about 8ft x 5ft (2.5m x 1.5m), and you should put down planks of wood on each side as walkways.

If you intend growing your water melons in a glasshouse or polythene growing tunnel, I recommend using raised beds approximately 12in (30cm) high. They should be sited on top of cultivated soil and filled with a mixture of 75 per cent peat, or composted materials, and 25 per cent soil. The additional height will help to retain moisture, enabling the plants to prosper on even the hottest days of the summer season.

A water melon weighing 262lb (117.9kg) was grown in 1990 by Mr B. Carson in Arrington, Tennessee, U.S.A.

Seeds

There are dozens of different varieties of water melon seeds available, both open-pollinated varieties and the much more expensive F1 hybrids. It is worth shopping around for the open-pollinated variety, which has the genetic capabilities to grow large water melons.

It is preferable to choose an open-pollinated variety of water melon seed when you are aiming to produce giants.

Sowing the seeds

Seeds can be sown from late spring. Sow each seed, with the curved end up and the slightly pointed end down, in a 3in (7cm) pot of peat-based

WATER MELON HAZARDS

RED SPIDER MITE is more liable to attack plants growing under glass or polythene, but in long spells of dry weather can also affect those growing outside. These tiny spiders are difficult to detect with the naked eye, and the first sign of an infestation may be when some of the plant's leaves turn yellow and become brittle. The leaves should be carefully removed and relegated to the dustbin, and the plant sprayed with a suitable insecticide immediately, and again three days later.

POWDERY MILDEW can greatly affect the performance of a water melon plant, and a severe attack will progressively reduce its vigour and eventually ruin the plant. This disease, identified by a white powdery covering to the plant's leaves, can be eliminated if treated with a suitable fungicide spray as soon as it is discovered.

GREY MOULD (Botrytis) is another common disease to affect water melons. It is usually caused by bad ventilation but will also infect any damaged part of a plant. To keep this fungus at bay, dead leaves and flowers must be removed from the plant every week. A spray with a fungicide mixture should eliminate the disease if it is treated in the early stages.

compost, and water thoroughly. Place the pots in a propagator with a heat setting of at least 75° F (24° C). If you do not have these facilities, cover each pot with a polythene bag secured with a rubber band, and place it beside your hot water tank. Germination will take fourteen to twenty days. Allow twenty to twenty-five weeks between seed-sowing and harvesting.

Transplanting

A vigorous water melon plant will produce on average eight large specimens, but if you are trying to grow a giant, it is best to limit the number to two.

Water melons grow much better on the plant's sub-laterals – the subsidiary side shoots that grow from the main laterals or side shoots of the plant. This is the method I recommend for producing strong sub-laterals: as each plant starts to develop, you should train the main growing stem in a straight line on the surface of the soil along one of the longer sides of the allocated growing area. When it reaches the end, pinch out the growing tip. The first lateral (side shoot) that appears on the main stem should be trained to grow at 90 degrees to it, and all other laterals which develop further along the stem should be removed as soon as they appear.

Once this first lateral has reached the boundary of the growing area, its growing tip should also be removed, and two of the sub-laterals which develop from this should be allowed to grow on to produce one water melon each. The length of these two fruit-bearing laterals can be governed by the space you have available, with a maximum of 10ft (3m) each. Any new side growths should be cut off from these two sub-laterals as they appear.

Pollination

Any female flowers which develop on the main runner or on the first lateral should be removed as soon as they appear, and those on the sub-laterals should be hand-pollinated. It is advisable to hand-pollinate all these female flowers as they open up until you are certain that you have pollinated one successfully. A female flower can be distinguished easily because it has a small water melon behind its petals, while the male has only a stem.

To pollinate the female flowers, cut a male flower from the plant, and carefully remove the petals. Then push the stamen full of pollen once or twice into the centre of the female flower. If pollination has been successful, in about seven

The leaves of a water melon plant have a distinctive shape but they are tender and vulnerable to pests and disease unless sprayed regularly.

days the small fruit which was already behind the female flower will start to grow.

Feeding

Water melons need a constant supply of water and nutrients. A daily feed of a very weak high nitrogen liquid fertilizer with a compound formula of 20N 10P 10K should be applied from ten days after transplanting until harvesting. The normally recommended feed diluted by ten will provide a suitable strength for daily use.

A foliar feed of the same mixture can also be used on the plants twice a week throughout the growing season.

Spraying

The leaves of water melon plants are tender, and should be sprayed every two weeks with an insecticide and fungicide mixture suitable for cucumbers. Begin spraying a week after transplanting and continue until harvesting. A few slug pellets and some insecticide powder should be sprinkled on the soil near the plants every three weeks.

Harvesting

A water melon should be left on the plant for as long as possible before it is weighed. If for any reason you do have to harvest it early, leave 2ft (60cm) of stem on either side of the stalk, and plunge these into a bowl of water to prevent dehydration.

To qualify for entry in the record books a water melon must be in a sound condition and free from dirt, soil and foreign bodies. The length of remaining stalk should not exceed 1in (2.5cm).

water melon chicken

4 chicken joints
½ pint (300ml) water
2 tablespoons sherry
salt
1 water melon, weighing about
10lb (4.5kg)

1. Put the chicken joints into a saucepan and pour over the water and sherry. Add salt and bring to the boil, then simmer for 30 minutes.
2. Remove a 'lid' from the water melon and scoop out enough flesh to make room for the chicken and cooking liquid.
3. Put in the chicken joints and cooking liquid, adding a little more salt, then replace the lid of the water melon and secure it with skewers.
4. Put the melon in a large pot of water and steam or simmer gently for 1½ hours, or until the skin of the melon turns yellow.
5. Try not to break the melon when serving as it is all delicious.

chapter eighteen

carrots and parsnips for length

Attempting to stretch nature to its limits has always been a fascinating challenge and it is not difficult to grow very long specimens – only a different growing method is required.

Although I have broken world records with a 16ft 10½ in (5.14m) carrot and a 14ft 3in (4.35m) parsnip, I still get the urge to do better. The seed sowing, feeding and spraying of long carrots and parsnips is the same as for heavy specimens although the growing methods will be significantly different.

Planning ahead

It would, of course, be impossible to grow vegetables of this length in the ground, and I recommend that you use 20ft (6m) lengths of plastic drainage pipes, 4in (10cm) in diameter. Each pipe should be attached to a 6ft (1.8m) high fence or building, with one end of the pipe 6in (15cm) below the top of it, and the other end resting on the ground. This should hold the pipe at an angle of approximately 30 degrees from the ground.

A carrot 202½ in (514.3cm) in length was grown by Bernard Lavery in Llanharry, South Wales.

Extra supports will be needed at 3ft (90cm) intervals to prevent the pipe from bending under the weight once it is filled with growing mixture.

When the pipe has been secured to the fence or wall, you must cut a 2in (5cm) strip from one end to the other. This will enable you to fill the pipe with growing mixture, water it, and harvest your vegetable with ease. To prevent the growing mixture being washed out of the pipe at watering time, a 6in (15cm) wide piece of soft mesh or cloth should be wrapped around the bottom of the pipe and secured.

The pipe can then be filled, starting from the bottom, with a growing mixture of one-third sand, one-third peat and one-third soil. You will need a stepladder for this operation once you reach halfway up the pipe. The whole length of the pipe should then be watered with a watering can and any settlement filled up with more growing mixture.

Seeds

When selecting seeds for growing long carrots and parsnips you should avoid the giant

The plastic drainage pipe is filled along its slit with a growing mixture of sand, peat and soil, starting at the bottom. A stepladder will be required to reach the top.

varieties (which are grown for their weight) and choose ones that have the genetic capabilities to grow long and slim. You should allow thirty-six to forty weeks from sowing seeds to harvesting your long 'giants'.

Seeds of both carrots and parsnips can be sown from early spring. They should be sown in the growing mixture at the top of each pipe in groups of twelve, ¼in (6mm) deep, and lightly watered. A polythene bag should then be tied over the end to create humidity. Carrot seed should germinate in approximately fourteen days, and parsnips in about twenty-four. As soon as this occurs the polythene bags should be removed. When the seedlings have

grown to a height of 2in (5cm), they should be thinned out very carefully, leaving only the strongest one to grow on.

Harvesting

Harvesting a long carrot or parsnip can take time, and may require a good deal of patience.

After watering the whole length of the pipe with a watering can, any settlement can be filled with more growing mixture before the seeds are sown.

The growing carrot or parsnip plant should be watered lightly, using a gentle spray from a hosepipe or an extension lance.

First, the cloth or mesh tied to the bottom end of the pipe must be removed, and a medium strength flow of water from a hosepipe directed into the bottom of the tube via the slit in its side. The growing mixture should be gradually washed down the tube to expose the roots, and

LONG CARROT AND PARSNIP HAZARDS

Apart from the usual pests and diseases which beset carrots and parsnips, long varieties grown in this way may also suffer from strong winds and birds. The foliage will benefit from some kind of wind shield, and a loose net covering the whole thing will prevent birds from scratching the compost and pecking at the roots.

great care must be exercised to avoid breaking off any of the hair-like taproots of either carrots or parsnips. These all count as part of the root system, and will add vital extra length when the specimen is measured.

Once all the growing mixture has been washed from the tube, the long roots should pull out easily, and should be wrapped in damp cloths before being transported to their destination.

To qualify for entry into the record books, a long carrot or long parsnip should be in a sound condition and must be measured in a straight line from the shoulder to the tip of the root.

Sow the carrot or parsnip seeds at the top of the pipe, ¼in (6mm) deep, in a group of twelve. After light watering, a polythene bag should be tied over the end to create humidity to aid germination.

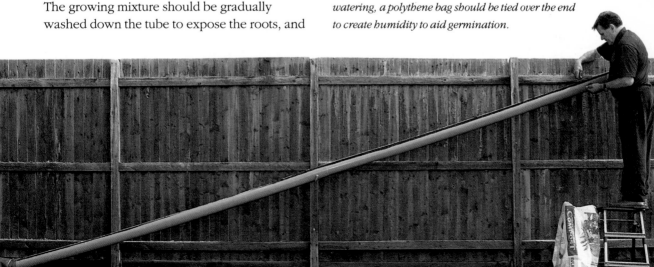

index

useful addresses

Worldwide Giant Seed Club
P.O. Box 63
Spalding
Lincolnshire PE11 1AA
England
(Will send seeds by mail order to any country
in the world: membership free)

Thompson & Morgan (Seeds) U.K. Ltd
Poplar Lane
Ipswich
Suffolk IP8 3BU

Thompson & Morgan Inc.
P.O. Box 1308
220 Farraday & Gramme Avenue
Jackson
N.J. 08527
U.S.A.

Thompson & Morgan SARL
La Melletiere
61150 St Ouen-sur-Maire
France

Page Seed Co.
Greene
N.Y. 13778
U.S.A.

Burpee Seeds
W. Atlee & Co.
Warminster
P.A. 18974
U.S.A.

World Pumpkin Confederation
14050 Gowanda State Road
Collins
New York 14034
U.S.A.

British National Pumpkin Society
23 Hawthorn Road
Llanharry
Pontyclun
South Wales CF7 9JD

W.P.C. Australia and New Zealand:
Wendy Stayner
35 Valley Road
Skye
Victoria
Australia

Algochimie S.A.
2.1. Nord
37110 Chateau-Renault
France